Ideology and Foreign Policy

Cyrco Press Series on
World and National Issues

IDEOLOGY AND FOREIGN POLICY
A GLOBAL PERSPECTIVE

edited with an introduction by
GEORGE SCHWAB

Cyrco Press, Inc., Publishers ● New York and London

Contents

Preface

On October 15 and 16, 1976, the second CUNY Conference on History and Politics was held at the Graduate Center of the City University of New York to examine the topic "Ideology and Foreign Policy." This volume contains the collected papers of that conference.

In organizing this conference acknowledgment is due to the Dean of Graduate Studies, Professor Hans J. Hillerbrand, for his unswerving support. I am grateful to his Executive Assistant, Mrs. Dorothy Weber, for the many suggestions she has made and for her most gracious help with the numerous details that are involved in organizing a gathering of this sort. This conference is also indebted to Professor Benjamin Rivlin, Dean of University and Special Programs, and to the Center for European Studies at CUNY.

For advice and encouragement I also wish to thank the members of the advisory committee of the CUNY Conference on History and Politics: Professors Henry Friedlander, Dankwart A. Rustow, Arthur M. Schlesinger, jr., and Joel H. Wiener.

For the editorial assistance received I would also like to thank Miss Edwina McMahon and, as usual, my gratitude goes to the editor of Cyrco Press, Ben Rosenzweig, for his patience and encouragement during the preparation of this volume. Naturally, I take the sole responsibility for anything that appears in this volume.

George Schwab
Director, CUNY Conference on
History and Politics

Introduction

The CUNY Conference on Ideology and Foreign Policy, the second in the series on History and Politics, is a continuation of the first gathering held in October 1974. It dealt with the question of detente.[1] Detente, which denotes the easing of tensions, has been an aim of American foreign policy for some time. But under the Nixon and Ford administration it became a cornerstone of our relations with Moscow.

The characterization of American foreign policy toward the Soviet Union as one of detente brought about much confusion because the concrete political realities did not appear to correspond to Washington's perception of East-West relations. The seeming disparity between fact and fancy led to a major debate among the articulate foreign policy publics in the United States. In the heat of discussion issues were derailed and the topic shrouded in mist. Hence the purpose of the CUNY conference was to cut through the fog that surrounded detente in order to probe whether the evidence did, in fact, support Washington's and also Moscow's contention that the word aptly reflected the essence of East-West relations.

Here we need not be detained by the details contained in the volume on detente, nor by all the developments that have

1

transpired since the conference. Nevertheless note must be made of the Helsinki agreement (1975). Among other things, it legalized the borders in Europe, thereby lending credence to the contention of those who argue that *Ostpolitik* has brought about genuine detente in the center of Europe.

This argument rests on the assumption that detente is divisible, namely, that it can exist in one area without necessarily existing in other areas. Although it is true that the two superpowers have so far successfully contained local flareups, thereby shielding the main course of U.S.-Soviet relations, this does not yet imply that detente is divisible. We need only be reminded of Locarno.

The treaties that were signed there in 1925 evoked, in the words of Sir Harold Nicolson, almost "hysterical jubilation."[2] It was widely and sincerely believed that the settlements in the west had brought genuine peace between France and Germany. As Germany had refused to recognize her eastern frontiers, the peace proved to be illusory and short lived. The proof of the indivisibility of detente came in September 1939. Translated to the current scene, what can be said is that *Ostpolitik* and Helsinki have enabled a focal point of tension to be shifted from the heart of Europe to other areas of the world. But this is as tantamount to detente as Nazi Germany's limiting air attacks on England while Hitler hurled his armed might against the Soviet Union.

Yet the question remains: Why has such an inherently positive and highly desirable policy not taken root and, therefore, not evolved? After all, both Washington and Moscow have proclaimed the necessity for genuine detente.

Light may be shed on this question now that the fog that surrounded detente has lifted considerably. The thrust of the second CUNY conference is derived from a question only briefly touched upon at the conference in 1974, one that may contain the key to the problem. It was asked whether political entities with fundamentally distinct conceptions of politics can genuinely coexist in the arena of world politics, for example, those states that base foreign policy on a secular or nonideological understanding of politics and those entities that contaminate it with ideology.

Ideology has to be distinguished here from propaganda. To degrade an actual or potential military adversary, a state built upon a secular or nonideological notion of politics does not hesitate to invoke in its propaganda battles such universal concepts as humanity, justice, progress, and so forth. Yet no matter how sanguine military confrontations between such states may be, wars are still largely waged within the framework of the *jus publicum Europaeum*.

The matter is different with totalitarian one-party states. A totalitarian movement's *raison d'être* is its *Weltanschauung*, which it considers all-embracing[3] and absolute. Once in power such a movement envelopes the state and attempts to penetrate its fiber to the last individual. Its aim is to synchronize the totality to the worldview being espoused.[4] Translated into foreign policy one must ask whether the foreign relations of totalitarian one-party states necessarily reflect their ideologies? The evidence shows that in the instance of Nazi Germany, for example, ideology was victorious over other considerations. A manifestation of this was the type of war that Hitler had ordered to be fought in the east. There he refused to be bound by the rules and regulations governing war.

Whether warring political entities conceive of military conflicts in enemy or foe terms,[5] and wage it accordingly, is not of immediate concern here, although the distinction can reflect a particular conception of politics. The question is: Can political entities with distinct notions of politics genuinely coexist? Given the contemporary political configuration, is it realistically possible, for example, to terminate the cold war and bring about genuine detente as is now the case between the United States and Japan and between France and West

Germany? To answer this question one must probe the interplay between politics and ideology in as many instances as possible to see if foreign policy decisions are direct emanations of ideology. If not, to what extent do the decisions made reflect the ideological climate of the countries involved?

Although not a new topic, the interplay between politics and ideology was pushed into the background with the ascendancy of a school of thought that is skeptical of the influence ideology exerts on foreign policy. According to this school, the propelling force in the world arena is the realistic interests of states. Power is the vehicle used to achieve these interests.[6] In this equation of power politics there is little room for ideology.[7]

Obviously, in the pursuit of what is commonly known as the interests of state the reality of power cannot be dismissed by any political entity. A rational pursuit of these interests can lead to a harmonious interplay of power. Conversely, the irrational ambitions of states can easily disturb whatever harmony is achieved. Here the dynamics of power act as brakes, that is, states that transgress certain acceptable limits or norms can often be forced to retreat to their proper bounds. Unless resources permit states to expand and to sustain the expansion, the politically realistic course is for states to accommodate themselves to the realities of power, even at the expense of what they may consider to be their interests.

All this is clear, including what happens when a harmonious interplay of power breaks down completely. What is not clear is the extent to which political entities with militant ideologies of a world scope are intent on subverting the norms under which nonideological states operate. Even more, to what extent are such totalitarian one-party states seriously intent on destroying one another and on challenging the very *raison d'être* of nonideological states?

Given the time limit of the conference one could not hope to answer every conceivable question. But on the assumption that the past can help shed light on the present, it was decided to treat the subject in historical perspective, that is, both Nazi Germany and Imperial Japan are included in the five case studies. If a learned discussion ensues, as it did in the instance of the detente gathering in 1974, the second CUNY conference will have accomplished its purpose.

NOTES

1. The proceedings of the conference have been published under the title *Detente in Historical Perspective*, ed. George Schwab and Henry Friedlander (New York, 1975; 2nd ed., 1978).
2. Harold Nicolson, *King George the Fifth: His Life and Reign* (London, 1952), p. 408.
3. This all-embracing quality is characterized by Karl Mannheim as the "total conception of ideology." *Ideology and Utopia: An Introduction to the Sociology of Knowledge,* trans. Louis Wirth and Edward Shils (New York, 1936), pp. 55-59.
4. Lewis S. Feuer [*Ideology and the Ideologists* (New York, 1975)] correctly notes that every ideology reflects the conviction that "politics must be based on philosophy" (p. 19), but hastens to add that ideology and philosophy are not identical. He observes that, among other things, an "ideology is an 'ism,'. . . a philosophical tenet which has been dissociated from the process of investigation and search, and has been affirmed as the axiom for a political group" (p. 188).
5. The conceptual distinction inherent in the words "enemy" and "foe," and some of its implications are discussed by George Schwab in "Enemy oder Foe: Der Konflikt der modernen Politik," trans. J. Zeumer, *Epirrhosis: Festgabe für Carl Schmitt,* ed. H. Barion et al. (Berlin, 1968), II, pp. 665-682. See also Ion X. Contiades, " 'ΕΧΘΡΟΣ' und 'ΠΟΛΕΜΙΟΣ' in der modernen politischen Theorie und der griechischen Antike," *Griechische Humanistische Gesellschaft,* Zweite Reihe (Athens, 1969), pp. 5ff.
6. For a discussion of political realism, see Hans J. Morgenthau, *Politics among Nations: The Struggle for Power and Peace,* 4th ed. (New York, 1967), pp. 3-14.
7. Not all power realists disregard the impact that power-alien ele-

ments, such as certain ideologies, play and have played in history. See John H. Herz, *Political Realism and Political Idealism: A Study in Theories and Realities* (Chicago, 1951), p. 29.

1.

Ideology and Foreign Policy in Historical Perspective
Vojtech Mastny

The marriage of ideology and foreign policy has been beset with problems, and our purpose here is to identify although not necessarily to solve them. In this undertaking, my particular task in opening the first session of the conference is to provide justification for the historical perspective that subsequent speakers will apply to specific cases. First, I shall consider briefly the origins of the problems, then, the relationship of ideology and power, and, finally, some of the patterns that show the influence of ideology on foreign policy.

In Anglo-American parlance, the very word ideology has an unsavory ring. For most people, it connotes either sinister goals dressed up in fancy phrases or, scarcely more reassuring, a starry-eyed devotion to abstractions incompatible with sound politics. But quite the opposite is true in the Soviet Union and elsewhere in the Communist world. There *ideinost*—emphatic conformity with ideology—has become an indispensable prerequisite of any policy worthy of that name.

Such strikingly different viewpoints are suggestive of the historic cleavage that has separated Western political cultures from those of eastern and central Europe. The Soviet worship of ideology derives, of course, from Marxist doctrine, specifically from its Hegelian ingredient. But a similar reverence has been characteristic also of much of German political thinking on which Hegel too left a decisive imprint. Indeed, the foremost authority on the phenomenon of ideology, Karl Mannheim, was himself a product of that tradition.

Much as cultural differences underlie the relationship between ideology and foreign policy, the characterization of these differences as a problem is nevertheless of relatively recent origin. Admittedly, ideologies have had an impact on international affairs for centuries—at any rate ever since Christian and Moslem rulers first attempted to spread their respective creeds abroad by force of arms. Still, only the emergence of mass politics and the growth of rapid communications enabled ideology to become the pervasive influence that is a landmark of our time. And only these developments have made the study of that influence a worthwhile scholarly undertaking.

Exactly when the "age of ideology" began depends very much on how broadly or narrowly the term is defined—and its definitions have been exceedingly flexible.[1] Similarly, opinions differ about whether that age is now dead—as has been pronounced so many times. There can be little doubt, however, that ideology, concerned with events in flux, is itself a historical category. As Hannah Arendt wrote, its concern is not with "something that *is* but [rather with] the unfolding of a process which is in constant change, . . . with becoming and perishing."[2]

It should be easier to determine when ideology first became a practical problem for statesmen and politicians. In this respect, the debate about the "new diplomacy" at the close of World War I was decisive in setting the terms on which international intercourse was to be conducted for decades to come.[3] René Albrecht-Carrié will have more to say about this controversy that is associated with the names of two famous ideologues, Wilson and Lenin. Their competition for the minds and hearts of the masses dramatized the importance of the adversary's ideological motivation—an issue that reached its climax a generation later at the time of the cold war.

The subsequent nuclear stalemate, coinciding with the abatement of East-West tensions, temporarily deprived ideology of much of its relevance to world realities. But things changed again with the rising doubts about the reliability of the "balance of terror" and about the genuineness of detente. Above all, the relentless expansion of Soviet military forces beyond any recognizable security needs calls for an explanation.[4] If, as critics of detente believe, Moscow has indeed embarked upon a quest for military superiority, does this development herald also a new drive for worldwide attainment of the ideological tenets of Marxism? Whatever the answer, it is appropriate that this conference on ideology and foreign policy should follow the conference on detente held on these premises two years ago.[5]

The question brings to the fore the relationship between ideology and power, or national interest—a relationship on which sharply divergent opinions have been recorded. They range from the conviction that the former is mere window-dressing for the latter to the belief that ideology can be a decisive political force in its own right.[6] But what really matters is that the distinction between ideological and power considerations is neither meaningless nor neat; in fact, its true meaning lies in its ambiguity.

Thus, for example, ideology in the past often initially served as camouflage, but gradually, even unwittingly as far as its proponents were concerned, it assumed a life of its own, that is, politicians succumbed to the creations of their own propaganda. What is more, among themselves as well they were disposed to express their goals and opinions in ideological language—as the Russians or the Chinese have been doing in their "esoteric communications."[7] And even if ideology did not motivate their goals, all the same it provided the vital conceptual framework for the perception and interpretation of the environment in which foreign policy is made.

Nor is the juxtaposition of ideology and national interest a simple matter. With respect to foreign affairs, nationalism may well be regarded as the ideology of national interest—a notion that would of course classify as ideological any policy giving absolute precedence to that interest. But even ardent nationalists have not always been clear in their minds about what is best for their nation. Its true interests could then clash with their ideological aspirations—as happened frequently in the Nazi case but, significantly enough, not nearly so often in the Soviet case.

This particular dissimilarity is indicative of the different patterns ideology may follow in influencing foreign policy. On the one hand, ideology has been conducive to the growth of aggressive authoritarian regimes with totalitarian pretensions. On the other hand, however, its impact on their international comportment has been anything but uniform. The variety is evident from the five examples most familiar from the recent past: Fascist Italy, Nazi Germany, Imperial Japan, Soviet Russia, and Maoist China.

Of the five, Fascist Italy has not been assigned a special place on the agenda of this conference, and justifiably so, for its ideology was both the most shallow and the most ineffective. To be sure, Mussolini was fond of boasting about the *tono fascista* that he insisted should pervade all of his regime's international dealings. But on closer look, this meant little more than a self-conscious display of bad manners that hampered the implementation of any policy.[8]

The Nazi ideology, although far from profound, was in contrast only too effective. This is not to say that its notorious compendium—Hitler's *Mein Kampf*—included a consistent blueprint for foreign policy. Rather, its ruminations provided the direction and, ironically enough, the seeds of the Nazis' undoing as well. For their ideology not only irresistibly led to aggression but also, as a fortunate built-in corrective, deprived its perpetrators of any realistic sense of priorities. Eloquent evidence will be presented in John H. Herz's paper.

During World War II there was much talk about the presumed ideological affinity of the Axis powers. Yet no ideology in fact compensated for the lack of common interests among them—a deficiency particularly evident in the hollow alliance between Germany and Japan. While ideological factors did figure in Japan's international posture, these only served to set it further apart from other nations. Arthur E. Tiedemann will provide fascinating details about this little known subject.

Unlike the three now defunct dictatorships, the Soviet Union and Maoist China are living rather than historic examples. Moreover, their official ideologies are neither superficial nor irrelevant to the conduct of foreign relations—features that make a historical appraisal difficult. Much more than the relatively short-lived Fascist regimes, the Communist ones have passed through several turbulent stages marked by policy reversals that may be liable to misinterpretation.

Despite these reversals, Soviet—and, to a smaller extent also, Chinese—diplomacy has nevertheless enjoyed a remarkably high reputation for effectiveness. And even adversaries have been willing to credit this result to the vigor and sense of purpose that Marxism imbues in its followers. But there is much to be said also for the opposite view, namely, that Communist leaders achieved what they did despite, rather than because of, lip service to their antiquated doctrine.

On at least two memorable occasions—during Stalin's Great Purge and during the Chinese Great Proletarian Cultural Revolution—apparent ideological considerations led to near demolition of the very tools of foreign policy. By the same token, the periods of the greatest Soviet advance—during the Stalin-Hitler pact, at the end of World War II, or arguably, since the advent of detente—have been those of ideological ebb. The inescapable conclusion is that ideologically motivated foreign policies are not necessarily more aggressive than those inspired by "mere" Realpolitik.

A final word remains to be said about foreign policy aimed at the preservation of the *status quo*—a goal that, in the opinion of detractors and defenders alike, has motivated the foreign policy of the United States. In his classic study, Mannheim stressed conservatives' fundamental aversion to ideology—a state of mind that causes them to develop one of their own only as a defense against the threat of an ideology seeking change.[9] Does this mean that a democratic ideology is peculiarly unsuited to provide inspiration in the realm of foreign affairs, and if so, is Realpolitik then the only alternative?

Raymond Aron once alluded to the dilemma inherent in the frequently heard exhortation to the West not to mix ideology and diplomacy—seemingly sensible advice that, however, amounts to giving its ideological adversaries a monopoly for inspiring goals.[10] But is there not something incompatible between "opting for wealth and opting for a crusade," as his two countrymen, Renouvin and Duroselle, suggested elsewhere in reference to the specific traditions that have shaped Western statesmanship? And they further noted: "The idea that the national interest can be served by promoting certain 'values'—a religion, an ideology—is found primarily among peoples who experienced crises of revolutionary fanaticism."[11]

Thus we are back again to the heritage of political culture pinpointed at the beginning of this paper. The impact of ideology on foreign policy is indeed predetermined by traditions and experiences independent of the individual statesman's will. But it is also an important part of the Western tradition to recognize the very definite room for free choice that still remains after all the determining factors have been accounted for. And it is precisely in this critical area that the historical view, ever challenged by the unique and the unpredictable rather than by the typical and the inevitable, offers the most rewarding perspective.

NOTES

1. The definition by John H. Herz is a good as any: "Ideology is the more or less coherent and consistent sum total of ideas and views on life and the world. . . that guides the attitudes of actual or would-be power holders." Davis L. Sills (ed.), *International Encyclopedia of the Social Sciences,* VIII (New York, 1968), p. 69.

2. Hannah Arendt, *The Origins of Totalitarianism* (Cleveland, 1958), p. 469.

3. Arno J. Mayer, *Political Origins of the New Diplomacy* (New York, 1969), pp. 368-393.

4. John Erickson, "Soviet Military Posture and Policy in Europe," in Richard Pipes (ed.), *Soviet Strategy in Europe* (New York, 1976), pp. 169-207.

5. George Schwab and Henry Friedlander (eds.), *Detente in Historical Perspective* (New York, 1975).

6. For representative examples, see Hans J. Morgenthau, *Politics among Nations: The Struggle for Power and Peace,* 4th ed. (New York, 1967), pp. 83-86, and Kurt London, *The Making of Foreign Policy* (Philadelphia, 1965), pp. 9-10.

7. William E. Griffith, "On Esoteric Communications: *Explication de texte,"* *Studies in Comparative Communism,* III (1970), pp. 47-60.

8. Gordon A. Craig, "Totalitarian Approaches to Diplomatic Negotiations," in A.O. Sarkissian (ed.), *Studies in Diplomatic History and Historiography* (London, 1961), pp. 108-113.

9. Karl Mannheim, *Ideology and Utopia: An Introduction to the Sociology of Knowledge,* trans. Louis Wirth and Edward Shils (New York, 1936), pp. 206-209.

10. Raymond Aron, *Peace and War: A Theory of International Relations* (New York, 1968), p. 600.

11. Pierre Renouvin and Jean-Baptiste Duroselle, *Introduction to the History of International Relations* (New York, 1967), pp. 272-273.

2.

Power Politics or Ideology? The Nazi Experience
John H. Herz

"Give me four years, and you will not recognize Germany any more." Thus spake Adolf Hitler in assuming control of Germany in 1933. The sentence was derisively chalked on the ruins of German cities by Allied soldiers in 1945. In producing this ruin of Germany and much of the world, what was the role of ideology, an ideology of racism, in contrast to "mere" power politics?

I define ideology as "the sum total of ideas and views on life and the world that guides the attitudes of actual or would-be power holders and/or movements"[1] and distinguish between general and international ideologies. The former—original Marxism would be an example—do not ordinarily pay much attention to international relations. The latter, on the other hand, are often internationalist and world revolutionary, such as that of the French Jacobins or the early Bolshevists.[2] These were idealist utopians, expecting the imminence of a golden age where peace and brotherhood among nations would prevail. When events prove them wrong, there usually is a radical turning away from the ideology to power politics. Then, as with Napoleon, *le jour de gloire est arrivé*, or, as with Stalin, the security and power of

14

one country becomes the overriding concern to which all other socialist movements must submit.

It is thus easy to make fun of ideologies that prove utopian as soon as their starry-eyed promoters try to carry them out in the real world. The same may be said about the Wilsonian pledge "to make the world safe for democracy."

But there is also an entirely different type of international ideology, a Social-Darwinistic one of the survival of the fittest, one that glorifies the power politics of one group, movement, nation, or race and aims at what is the exact opposite of the idealist utopians' objectives, namely, domination, and possibly the world hegemony, of one country or race. Of this, Hitlerism is the supreme example.

But if power, domination, and expansionism are at the core of an ideology like Hitler's, the question arises: What distinguishes a foreign policy thus motivated from the so to speak "normal" power policies of expansionist rulers like an Alexander's, a Frederick's, or the early Bismarck's? The problem of distinguishing between policies of the national interest, expansionistically interpreted, and ideologically motivated policies here becomes a sticky one. Was not the role of Nazi ideology almost identical with the glorification of expansionist power politics that characterized traditional imperialist foreign policy that oftentimes was also Social Darwinist and even racist?

In such cases, I submit, ideological and political power motivations can be distinguished only if it can be shown that (a) the pursuit of power and national interest was, at least at times, subordinated to a power-damaging ideological policy, and (b) the conduct of foreign policy in peace and the conduct of war reveal the specific impact of ideology, distinguishing it from that conducted by normal powers. It is the thesis of this paper that in the Nazi case, perhaps in contrast to most other movements and ideologies of our time, ideology prevailed whenever ideological considerations and objectives clashed with those involving national interests.

I

Nazi ideology was Hitler's ideology. To the very end he did not permit anybody, including his closest aides, to interpret it in any way that would deviate from his doctrine. Whenever—as happened from time to time—he did not reveal (or, perchance, himself was not sure of) the consequences of his doctrine in detail, there developed conflict and rivalry among subleaders and chaos in policy. Some examples will be furnished later. As for the grand outlines of his doctrine, not much need be said here: It is all in *Mein Kampf.* It is an ideology of extreme nationalism and racism. Nature, so it is alleged, has divided mankind into superior—culture creating—and inferior racial groups. Only the vaguely defined Aryans are creative and thus worthy of dominating the inferior ones. Germanic groups have created all high civilizations, such as that of Greek antiquity, and founded states, such as old Russia. But racial mixture, time and again, led to their degeneration and, therewith, the fall of civilizations. Thus it was the mission of Germans and their Führer to ensure the purity of the Germanic race and to secure for it living space. By some miraculous happenstance, that space was available in the east. World Jewry, eternal enemy of all superior races and nations, had weakened the substance of the Russian nation by establishing its control under the guise of Bolshevism. Russia's formerly ruling Germanic element had been destroyed, and so its vast spaces were now open to German settlement. Anybody in the way of such settlement was to be Germanized (if found to be of Germanic origin), or used as slave labor, or physically exterminated. Those of superior racial origin who were hostile to German expansion would, as the most dangerous elements, be liquidated, while their offspring would be taken away to be Germanized. Only when a Greater Germany was in control of all of Europe could its future be considered safe. But this was not to be the end. Hitler, according to a quote by Rudolf Hess from as early as 1927, believed that world peace could come only "when one power, the racially best one, has attained complete and uncontested world supremacy." It would then establish a world police, with the lower races "restricted accordingly."[3]

Before turning east, Germany had to defeat France. Britain, until it too came under German control, was a natural ally, but Hitler's attitude toward the English was always—to quote one of the foremost students of Nazi foreign policy— "a mixture of admiration and hate, never entirely untangled."[4] There was admiration of its empire, its capacity to control, through a small number of especially bred Englishmen, huge Indian masses, but Jewish influence threatened degeneration. Actually, at the time of Operation Sea Lion, i.e., the planned invasion of Britain, an enemy list of some 2,700 persons had been prepared, "ranging from Winston Churchill and Charles de Gaulle to H. G. Wells and Virginia Woolf";[5] Hitler was not one to be afraid of Virginia Woolf! The Japanese were "racially uncreative" but clever. The Americans were at first admired not only because of their Nordic elements but also because they had managed to control a vast Lebensraum; but subsequently Hitler considered the United States fatally weakened through racial mixture with Jews and Negroes. The French were likewise beyond redemption; they had become mongrelized. Besides, like other originally healthy nations, they were the victims of "supranational forces," like Free Masonry, political Catholicism, Bolshevism, and, above all, and again and again, international Jewry. Emphasis on a Jewish conspiracy to destroy healthy races through despoiling and then controlling them assumed ever increasing importance in Hitler's phantasies. There was a friend-foe relationship between the Aryan-Nordic groups and the Jews. The thrust of Nazi propaganda was against "Jewish Bolshevism"; Bolshevism was "the highest stage of Judaism"; Bolshevism had become identical with Zionism.[6]

Considering the Jewish holocaust and the millions of other victims of Hitler's policies, few doubt today that Hitler, from the very beginning of his assumption of power in 1933, consistently pursued aims based on the mad ideology of *Mein Kampf*. But because there are still some, like A.J.P. Taylor, who believe that, once in power, he started out with moderate objectives, only to be led step by step, and sometimes against his own expectations, from one to another of his bolder ventures, it is necessary briefly to describe the reality, which was one of the boldest and most successful cases of dissemblance and deception in history. Abundant documentation is now available to prove this. Just listen to what Nazi leaders, such as Goebbels, admitted after simulation was no longer necessary:

> Until now we have succeeded in leaving our opponents in the dark about the real goals of Germany, just as our domestic opponents did not know what we were aiming at until 1932 and that our oath of legality was only a stratagem. We wanted to gain power through legal means, but we did not intend to use it legally. . . . They could have destroyed us but they did not. . . . It was exactly the same with foreign policy. In 1933 a French minister-president should have said: The man who wrote *Mein Kampf* has become Reich chancellor. Such a man cannot be tolerated as a neighbor. Either he goes or we march. That would have been thoroughly logical. But it was not done. They left us alone, *they allowed us to slip through the danger zone,* and when we were ready, well armed, better than they, they started the war. (Goebbels to the German press in April 1940—the only Goebbels' lie here being the word "they" instead of "we" in referring to having started the war.)[7]

Thus all those post-1933 speeches about peace, all those assurances of merely wanting to revise the Versailles Treaty to attain justice and equality for Germany, all those doctrines about the natural rights of each nation and the genuine role of international law were pure eyewash, a systematic policy of concealment, a grandiose game of camouflage to make Hitler appear "harmless" (Selbstverharmlosung—as the foremost German historian of Nazi foreign policy has put it.)[8] Hossbach and similar documents prove forever the same. Thus, in another secret talk to the press in 1938, Hitler himself admitted that circumstances had compelled him for five years to talk peace but that from now on the German press had to make it clear to the German people that certain tasks could only be solved by force.[9] Indeed, as early as 1933, in a talk to his generals, he was frank in his insistence on Lebensraum and expansion, debunking the Geneva system while stressing the necessity to gain superior strength through rearmament.[10] Thus, in referring to Taylor's assertion that Hitler was not an ideologist but a pure opportunist, a manipulator of power like any traditional diplomat, Gerhard Weinberg correctly states that "opportunism was in fact an integral part of his long-term theory of political action. . . . New evidence, as it comes to light, not only fits but in astonishing ways underlines the accuracy of this view."[11] The great appeaser was not Chamberlain but Hitler himself! Even toward Stalin: In June 1940, he told his generals that, if Britain was ready to make peace, his hands would become free "for the real task, the destruction of Bolshevism," and planning for the Russian campaign began during the heyday of Stalin-Hitler friendship.[12] I may perhaps not be immodest in priding myself on having discovered this grandiose camouflage play at an early point in the writings of Nazified German international lawyers who loyally fulfilled their assigned task of providing the theoretical underpinning of Hitler's "peace policy" for the deception of Western opinion,[13] but my book appeared in 1938, at the time of Munich, when nobody listened.

Thus it all amounted, to quote Weinberg again, to a "combination of long-range planning with opportunism in detail, of a fanatically held goal with a flexibility of means."[14] But this could be said of other power politicians. What we must now ask is: Was the goal defined by considerations of power and national interest or, when these clashed with ideological objectives, did the ideology prevail?

II

Some major policy decisions seem to point toward conflicting answers. Thus, on the one hand, we have Hitler's war with racially "Germanic" Britain and his alliance with a certainly not quite Aryan Japan; does this not prove that the ideology of racism was mere subterfuge and power politics was predominant? On the other hand, does not his final defeat, caused primarily by taking on the Russians and the Americans, prove neglect of political power considerations? But power politics may likewise fail. Thus we have to dig into the details of policies to find the answer.

To me the evidence of the prevalence of ideology over interest is overwhelming. The final solution of the Jewish question, i.e., the holocaust, with its deportations and mass killings that lasted to the very end when the war was clearly lost and Hitler's troops were retreating everywhere, was only the best known and the most conspicuous and horrible among the policies of annihilation and population transfers that, especially in the east and southeast of Europe, were carried out at whatever cost wherever the Nazis attained control over new areas and the SS Einsatzgruppen had done their bloody work of sorting out Jews and others singled out for immediate liquidation. Thus, after the initial Polish campaign and the extermination of the Polish elite (nobility, clergy, intellectuals) and other groups (referred to by Hitler as "Jews, Polacks, and other trash—Juden, Polacken, und andres

Gesindel," including gypsies), Germanization proceeded through Himmler's "Reich Commissariat for the Strengthening of Germandom" by settling Germanic elements in the Warthegau, former Polish areas incorporated into Germany. Subsequently vast numbers of others deemed racially German were shifted there for agricultural settlement, while millions of Poles were dumped into rump Poland where Governor Hans Frank, complaining bitterly about having to deal with the trash, had to see that they were either used as slave labor or else liquidated. As everywhere else, the difficulties of racially examining every single person led to big muddles and great economic loss. To quote the historian of these events, Norman Rich, the result "was a disastrous decline in production," with many of the evacuees eventually joining guerrilla forces, with crops burned, livestock killed, and so forth.[15] Yet Himmler, backed, as always, by Hitler, insisted on continuing these policies in the teeth of such adverse economic and political consequences. Hitler "refused to sanction the use of Polish forces . . . and to the end backed up the measures of his racial extremists"[16] even when, after Katyn, some Poles seemed ready to fight the Russians.

The same of course was true during the Russian campaign.[17] There, especially in the Baltic and the Ukraine, Germans were first greeted as liberators. But although not only generals but other high Nazi aides, such as Rosenberg, advocated the at least temporary use of pro-German elements and suggested deferring "final solutions" until after the war, Hitler, with savage fanaticism and complete disregard of political, military, and economic consequences, insisted on putting his idea of the "New Order" into practice immediately, this way transforming a population ready to welcome the Germans as liberators from Stalin's yoke "into a people inspired with determination more fanatic then that of the Nazis themselves, because more desperate."[18] Vlassov came too late and proved inefficient. Hitler, on the basis of his racial ideology, had expected Bolshevized Russia to break down quickly before his onslaught. But even when the war dragged on for years, he stated and restated his triad of objectives—extermination, enslavement, German settlement—with undiminished obstinacy. A speech to army group commanders in July 1943 "might have been delivered in July 1941—or in 1924."[19] Resettlement of Germanic types by the hundreds of thousands continued right into 1944.[20] According to an order by Heydrich, "in dealing with the Jewish problem, economic necessities are to be ignored in principle."[21] Their mass executions went on, "unconcerned by the fact that they had been manufacturing arms and clothing for the Wehrmacht."[22] Himmler was less concerned "with getting men and supplies to the front than with the mass shifting of peasants, their livestock, equipment, and household goods from one end of Europe to another and carrying out his massive racial resettlement program," employing "thousands of able-bodied men through the war to determine the racial background of conquered peoples."[23]

While it is possible that this program, even with its vast waste of manpower and provisions, its alienation of potential friends, and its creation of fanatical resistance, by itself did not suffice to lose Hitler his war, it certainly proves the victory of ideology—or madness if you prefer—over more rational considerations of power and interest policies.

In eastern Europe Nazi ideology at least furnished some applicable standards; even greater confusion about the implementation of the racial doctrine is found when we turn to other parts of Europe. Thus in the Balkans, Slavonic groups that one would not have thought of in this respect, such as Slovenes and Croats, were considered suitable for Germanization, with the result that the Serbs from their areas were dumped into rump Yugoslavia under especially cruel conditions, causing the large-scale partisan warfare that tied down Hitler's forces to the end; orders to execute one hundred

natives for every German killed only stimulated resistance.[24]
In the north and west, Hitler's particular racial ideology created friction even with fascist minded groups and leaders, the
"Quislings" in the individual and generic senses. Thus Mus-
sert, the Dutch Nazi leader, or Flemish leaders in Belgium,
dreamed of a Greater Netherland, or Grossdietsches Reich,
which, together with a similar Scandinavian league, would
form a group of people closely allied with, but not an integral
part of, Hitler's own Greater Germany. But Hitler's aim was
not to have Grossdietsche or other Reiche but one Gross-
deutsches Reich controlled by the master race, that is, to
incorporate all racially related people into the Reich. This,
however, antagonized his non-German Nazi friends and in
practice not only meant difficulties in controlling these areas
but also disappointing results in the recruitment of SS groups
of Flemings, Walloons, and others for the fight in the east.[25]
With regard to the major part of France Hitler never could
make up his mind, but Alsace, Lorraine, and some northern
sections were up for Germanization, again with all the costs
and waste of population shifts, with land remaining unculti-
vated, transportation systems overworked, and so forth.[26]
Here, too, Hitler's and Himmler's ideological extremism
worked to the disadvantage of the primary goal: winning a
war.

III

If so far I have not talked about the conduct of foreign
affairs—not even mentioned a foreign minister's name—this
simply reflects the fact that, during the war, decisions were
made and implemented not by a Ribbentrop or other members of the foreign office but by the Führer himself as well as
by the leader and subleaders of the SS (unless Hitler, who
even there usually made the top decisions, left military matters to the generals). Germany had become an SS state. Be-

fore the outbreak of the war, as we have seen, policy was one of simulation and camouflage, with the foreign policy apparatus, taken over from pre-Hitler times and little revamped, faithfully carrying out a policy that, ostensibly, fitted in with the conservative-nationalist-revisionist attitudes of most of its staff, although many must have recognized its function of deception.

But as in every totalitarian regime whose aim is expansion, there developed, right from 1933 on, that two-track system of conducting affairs in which official and normal relations are kept up through the traditional apparatus of the foreign office and the foreign service while, side by side with it, partly above ground and partly covertly, ideologically motivated relations are taken up with groups and counterparts abroad; for example: the members of the Comintern in their relations not with the Soviet government but with the CPSU. In the Nazi Fascist case this second-track policy led to the undermining of systems and countries programmed for subsequent conquest or takeover, to Trojan-horse tactics, fifth columnism, and so forth. However, because Hitler, during the first four or five years, engaged in a policy of camouflage, second-track activities similarly had to be camouflaged, which led to great complication, confusion, in-fighting among groups and leaders in Germany and abroad—in short, a policy that cannot be characterized as having been very effective in most instances.[27] Time and again, overenthusiastic foreign and domestic leaders had to be disavowed in order not to disturb first-track, normal relations too severely. The activities of the Bund in the United States can serve as an example. Henlein in Czechoslovakia, or Austrian Nazis (the latter especially after the debacle of 1934) at first had to play the role of "loyal" citizens of their respective countries, only to reveal their true colors when the time was ripe. Occasionally Hitler would even officially disavow foreign pro-Nazi groups in order to maintain the friendship of an official ruler (e.g.,

Rumanian dictator Antonescu versus the Fascist Iron Guard).

By and large, during the first years, foreign organizations were chiefly used for three purposes: (a) nazification of German citizens abroad, (b) influencing those of German origin or descent who were foreign citizens, (c) propagandizing the rest of the population and in this way preparing for the day when, in Europe, one would start expansion; outside Europe, for the day one would need friendly or at least nonhostile attitudes. Successful cases were Austria and Czechoslovakia in 1938. Elsewhere, however, there frequently reigned total confusion over aims and strategies, rivalry, and often open hostility among the many organizations, within and outside Germany, established to deal with these matters and mutually contesting each other's jurisdictions. There was a proliferation of offices, the office of Rosenberg, the office of Ribbentrop (until he was appointed foreign minister), the office of the deputy party leader Hess and under him, Gauleiter Bohle who was in charge of the AO, Auslandsorganisation, or foreign organization of the party, and so on and so forth. Because Hitler, as so often was the case, hesitated to intervene in jurisdictional conflicts (which gave him a chance to play off one group or leader against another or others), the result was not only that matters were handled by amateurish people in amateurish fashion but also that, eventually, it was again Himmler and Heydrich, with their Vomi or Volksdeutsche Mittelstelle (Office for Racial Germans Abroad) who won out over all the others.[28] Here, too, the SS state had achieved ascendency.

There were few in the old, pre-Nazi establishment who did not play along. Only one ambassador (in Washington) resigned when Hitler assumed control. Von Neurath, foreign minister until the era of simulation ended in 1938, never proved an obstacle. Subsequently, as Reich Protector in Prague, he played the role of figurehead, leaving power and dirty work to Sudeten Nazi Karl Frank, and, subsequently, to

Heydrich. After the invasion of Poland, when the military
became aware of the murderous activities of the SS forma-
tions in the areas behind the front, there was little protest
and no resistance, although the actions created some unrest
even among ordinary German soldiers who could not all be
prevented from observing what was going on. There is a revealing document by Heydrich that showed that the generals,
who had first assured the Polish population that the laws of
war would be observed, believed that the illegal SS activities
were unauthorized. But commander-in-chief Blaskowitz, after
protesting to Hitler, got the answer: "With salvation army
methods one cannot conduct a war." Blaskowitz was dismissed soon thereafter. To a small circle of military and party
leaders who had complained about the "bad image" created
by what they considered "excesses," Himmler admitted that
the mass executions of thousands of the Polish intelligentsia
had been ordered by Hitler personally, although, toward the
outside, he, Himmler, had to take the rap. Said he: "We had
to have the stamina—you shall hear this but right away forget
it again—to shoot thousands of leading Poles";[29] and: "I
don't do anything that is not known to the Führer." Hitler
himself declared that "the army should be glad to be rid of
this responsibility." And Frank, governor-general in Poland,
who had complained that others, not knowing of Hitler's
orders, considered him and the SS murderers, had to console
himself with these words of the Führer: "And you, my dear
Frank, have to finish your devil's job in Poland to the end."
Which he, Frank, did.[30]

Another document that came to light after the war[31]
shows the futility of the efforts of those very few who, from
the vantage point of some official positions, tried to do something to have the rules of war observed and to prevent their
worst violations. Graf Moltke, subsequently executed as a
member of the German resistance, from his desk in the international law section of the Supreme Command of the Army,

tried to explain the law to his superior officers, only to be told that what he wrote was "lawyer's junk" and "theoretical scribbling," and that his job was to provide legal justification for whatever was done. Frustrated in most of his efforts, he complained (in private, of course) bitterly about the Hitler-enthrallment (Hitler-Hörigkeit) of most generals. He continued to consider it his duty to warn but realized his impotence: "Unfortunately, it is of no use, but at least we have saved our honor." For that he paid with his life.

In contrast to Poland, when the Russian campaign began, and in the face of declared Soviet readiness to observe the rules of war on PWs and so forth, Hitler's instructions to the military were right away quite unequivocal. This was to be "no ordinary war but a life-and-death struggle between two races and two ideologies; between German and Slav; between National Socialism and the criminal code of Jewish Bolshevism." Therefore soldiers were "not to be bound by laws of war, nor was there any room for chivalry. . . . The Bolshevist-Jewish intelligentsia and all Communist political leaders were to be wiped out, and the war of extermination was to be waged with unprecedented, unmerciful, unrelenting harshness." There were to be no regular military courts; political leaders, hostile civilians, and others were to be summarily executed.[32] No writings or documents revealing objections by German academic international lawyers have ever come to light. In contrast to Moltke, they survived (and, for the most part, reoccupied their chairs after the war).

Thus ideology prevailed throughout, and we can sum it up, with Norman Rich, by stating that Hitler "remained true to his principles, which constituted fundamental guidelines for his political conduct from the time he emerged from his prison at Landsberg in 1924 to his death in the rubble of Berlin."[33] Deviations, such as the Stalin-Hitler Pact, as we have seen, were short-lived stratagems. And other major decisions, such as the one to wage war with Russia, or to declare war on the United States, can at least partly be explained by an ideology that fatally underestimated the power of the former and the power potential of the latter. These were prime examples of "cognitive dissonance," resolved in favor of ingrained doctrine. If ever, in history, ideology had world-shaking consequences, it had them in the case of Hitlerism.

IV

I would like to take this occasion at the end of my academic career, during which much of my research has been devoted to the role of the territorial state and power politics, to reformulate in the light of the foregoing a few of my conclusions which—so it now appears to me—like similar ones of my colleagues, have been the products of an however unconscious or unadmitted ideology of the alleged deep contrast between the so-called normal conduct of foreign affairs and the role of the classical nation state system, on the one hand, and ideologically motivated policies of totalitarian or otherwise "deviant" regimes, on the other hand.

We have been wrong, I submit, in celebrating the limited wars (what Carl Schmitt has called the *gehegte Krieg*) conducted under the principles of the balance of power and the restraining rules of the *jus publicum Europaeum* after the Westphalian Peace, contrasting them with the total wars conducted by or against totalitarian powers in our century. I have been wrong in evaluating overly positively the protecting function of the territorial state domestically and its stabilizing and balancing functions in international relations. At best, these have been trends promoted by liberal democratic ideology but only rarely put into practice. Thus, as far as limited war is concerned, listen to what Voltaire, observing the campaigns of Frederick the Great, had to say:

> Nothing could be smarter, more splendid, more brilliant, better drawn up than the two armies. Trumpets, fifes, haut-

boys, drums, cannons formed a harmony such as has never been heard even in hell. The cannons first of all lay flat about six thousand men on each side; then the musketry removed from the best of worlds some ten thousand blackguards who infested its surface. The bayonet also was the sufficient reason for the death of some thousands of men. The whole might amount to some thirty thousand souls. Candide, who trembled like a philosopher, hid himself as well as he could during this heroic butchery. At last, while the two kings each commanded a Te Deum in his camp, Candide decided to go elsewhere to reason about effects and causes. He clambered over heaps of dead and dying men and reached a neighboring village, which was in ashes; it was an Abare village which the Bulgarians had burned in accordance with international law. Here, old men dazed with blows watched the dying agonies of their murdered wives who clutched their children to their bleeding breasts; there, disemboweled girls who had been made to satisfy the natural appetites of heroes gasped their last sighs; others, half-burned, begged to be put to death. Brains were scattered on the ground among dismembered arms and legs. Candide fled to another village as fast as he could; it belonged to the Bulgarians, and Abarian heroes had treated it in the same way. Candide, stumbling over quivering limbs or across ruins, at last escaped from the theater of war. . . .[34]

Yes, you may object, this was the eighteenth century, but what about the nineteenth, with its progress toward more humanitarian rules and behavior patterns? It was so humanitarian that it was the horrible suffering of the uncared-for wounded and dying of one of its bloody battles that moved Henri Dunant to set up the International Red Cross organization. The Hague Conventions subsequently codified its and other laws of warfare. But these rules were never observed in areas "beyond the line" where European or other Western powers slaughtered natives freely;[35] that is, in colonial warfare, that, involving "superior" and "inferior" races, reflected that same Social-Darwinistic attitude out of which Hitler's own philosophy grew, whether it was the genocidal annihilation of the Indians by the American whites, or King Leopold's Congo wars, or the Herero tribes eradicated by the Germans, or North African Berbers exterminated by the French. And in that civilized nineteenth century Social Darwinism was by no means limited to the relations of Europeans or of whites to non-Europeans. Thus the British revealed stereotypes toward the Irish resembling those of the whites toward the blacks in the United States. Opined Punch: "The Irish are the missing link between the gorilla and the Negro."[36]

True, some of the Hague rules were observed in World War I, but the slaughter of millions in an insane trench warfare was not in violation of these rules.[37] Out of that blood bath emerged young people who, like Adolf Hitler, came to glorify the heroic nature of mechanized warfare, determined to repeat it for the final victory of the most heroic race. Those who drew the opposite conclusion from the catastrophe of that war failed in their attempts to create a system ensuring international peace through collective security[38] and, domestically, to establish a more just society. Although slavery had yielded to emancipation, social justice and a fair distribution of national wealth, on the whole, have remained aspirations rather than achievements, even in affluent nations like America, and the same, by and large, is true of the protection of basic rights and liberties in the territorial state. It turns out, after the recent revelations about police-state trends in the United States, that the chief difference between their total suppression in totalitarian countries and their disregard in the so-called Free World is that in the latter we can still read about it in the *New York Times* and protest.[39] The trend has been toward the emergence of a kind of state within the state domestically, and, in international relations, toward a two-track system in the conduct of foreign affairs by democratic nations, reminding one ominously of that of the Soviets or the Nazis. Listen to what Nixon had to say about this:

> Because the CIA's covert activity in supporting Mr.
> Allende's political opponents might at some point be dis-
> covered, I instructed the American embassy in Chile not to
> be involved. I did this so that the American embassy could
> remain a viable operation regardless of the outcome of the
> election.[40]

Planned assassination of foreign rulers had no parallel even in
the eighteenth century (when corrupting them was the preferred method), but was preceded by fascist action of this
type in the 1930s.[41] Atrocities committed in Vietnam vie
with Hitler's war crimes. Genocide was not an invention of
the Nazis but had its precedent in the Armenian massacres
which, because they happened during World War I, were
hardly noticed at the time (except by Hitler who later
claimed that, after all, the Turks had done it before); by now,
it has become the fashion all over the place, whether in East
Bengal, Burundi, or Indonesia.

In this country the ideology of anti-Communism has
meant assuming the very coloration of the opponent. And
what is most frightening is the general apathy in the face of it
all, resulting, among other things, in the nonprosecution of
those in the government who violate the law by illegally in-
terfering with citizens' rights and liberties. It is the hallmark
of the Rechtsstaat that government criminality is dealt with
under that state's own rules and procedures, but it rarely
happens, here and elsewhere, that members of so-called law
enforcement agencies, for instance, or of the military, or of
the intelligence services, are tried and punished for their
transgressions. True, Hitler was more of a genius in the organization and execution of atrocities, and the results, to be
sure, are never to be forgotten or forgiven. But the trend has
been in the same direction everywhere. We have underestimated society's (all societies') capacity for aggression, greed,

cowardice, and human incapacity to be impressed, morally or even for reasons of mere survival, by the excesses of totalitarian regimes. The effect of Hitler's holocaust, for instance, has not been the disappearance of anti-Semitism but its resurgence. Terror and antiterror prevail, and the torture of political opponents, in Gestapo-like fashion, has become the daily practice all over the world, including the "Free World." As one remarked shortly after the war, there is "ein Hitler in uns selbst" (a Hitler in most of us). And thus we must, sadly, agree with Bert Brecht who said, after Nazism, the war, and the holocaust were over, "Der Schooss ist fruchtbar noch der dies gebar" ("The womb is fertile still which gave birth to that"), the "that" referring to Adolf Hitler.

NOTES

1. See "International Relations: Ideological Aspects," in *International Encyclopedia of the Social Sciences*, vol. 8, pp. 69ff.

2. On this, and especially the surprising similarities of the two ideologies mentioned, see my *Political Realism and Political Idealism* (Chicago, 1951), pp. 78ff., 88ff.

3. Gerhard L. Weinberg, *The Foreign Policy of Hitler's Germany, Diplomatic Revolution in Europe, 1933-1936* (Chicago, 1970), pp. 2ff. Weinberg's is one of three works that, incredibly rich in material and source references, deal exhaustively with Nazi ideology, foreign policy, and actions in as well as policies toward the occupied countries. The two other ones are: Norman Rich, *Hitler's War Aims*, vol. 1, *Ideology, the Nazi State, and the Course of Expansion* (New York, 1973), vol. 2, *The Establishment of the New Order* (New York, 1974), and Hans A. Jacobsen, *Nationalsozialistische Aussenpolitik, 1933-1938* (Frankfurt-Berlin, 1968). The analysis of this paper is chiefly based on these three works. From now on, whenever directly quoted, they will be referred to simply as Weinberg, Rich, and Jacobsen, respectively.

4. Weinberg, p. 15.

5. Rich, vol. 2, p. 398.

6. Jacobsen, pp. 445ff.

7. Rich, vol. 1, p. 266; slightly different German text in Jacobsen, p. 617. Emphasis supplied. Here is one example of how very few—in

this case, a discerning poet and writer—realized at an early point how the Nazis were "slipping through the danger zone." In March 1934, Hermann Hesse wrote to Thomas Mann: "... the whole situation looks very serious, for there is no doubt that they are heavily rearming. I hardly know what I would want or decree if I were obliged for a minute to direct history—I almost think I would have the French march across the Rhine and make Germany lose a war which in a few years it may win." *The Hesse-Mann Letters: The Correspondence of Hermann Hesse and Thomas Mann, 1910-1955,* Anni Carlsson and Volker Michels, eds. (New York, 1975), p. 35.

8. Jacobsen, p. 445.

9. Jacobsen, p. 333.

10. Weinberg, pp. 26f.

11. Weinberg, pp. 1f.

12. Rich, vol. 1, pp. 160, 162, 209.

13. See Eduard Bristler (i.e., John H. Herz), *Die Völkerrechtslehre des Nationalsozialismus* (Zürich, 1938), passim.

14. Weinberg, p. 355.

15. Rich, vol. 2, p. 83; see also, more generally, *ibid.,* pp. 74ff., 80ff.

16. Rich, vol. 2, p. 100 and footnote 116 on p. 40l.

17. On this see, for details as well as for the general thesis of the great impact of ideology on policies, the by now classical rendering by Alexander Dallin, *German Rule in Russia, 1941-1945, A Study of Occupation Policies* (New York, 1957), passim.

18. Rich, vol. 1, p. 249.

19. Rich, vol. 2, p. 330; see also, more generally, *ibid.,* pp. 326-275.

20. Rich, vol. 2, p. 357.

21. Rich, vol. 2, p. 352.

22. Rich, vol. 1, p. 58.

23. Rich, vol. 1, pp. 57f.

24. Rich, vol. 2, pp. 272ff., 293; on Czechoslovakia, see Rich, vol. 2, pp. 27ff., and Vojtech Mastny, *The Czechs under Nazi Rule* (New York and London, 1971).

25. Rich, vol. 2, pp. 155, 191.

26. Rich, vol. 2, pp. 208, 237.

27. On this, and especially on the "double-track tactics" and their effects, see Weinberg, passim (innumerable examples), as well as Jacobsen, pp. 246, 453, 598ff.

28. Jacobsen, p. 609; on the development of the organizational setup, see Jacobsen, passim.

29. During the Watergate coverup this kind of thing was referred to as "deniability."

30. See Helmut Krausnick, "Hitler und die Morde in Polen," *Viertel-jahrshefte für Zeitgeschichte,* vol. 11, 1963, pp. 196ff. and document there reprinted.

31. Published in *Vierteljahrshefte für Zeitgeschichte,* vol. 18, 1970, pp. 14ff., with comments by Ger Van Roon.

32. Rich, vol. 1, pp. 212f.

33. Rich, vol. 1, p. xiii.

34. See the first three paragraphs of chapter 3, as translated in *Candide and Other Writings,* Modern Library edition (New York, 1956), p. 114.

35. On these "amity lines," beyond which the Hobbesian *homo homini lupus* situation prevailed, see Carl Schmitt, *Der Nomos der Erde im Völkerrecht des Jus Publicum Europaeum,* 2nd ed. (Berlin, 1974), pp. 60ff.

36. See Richard Ned Lebow, *White Britain and Black Ireland, The Influence of Stereotypes on Colonial Policy* (Philadelphia, 1976), p. 40. According to *Punch,* Irishmen were by their very nature the laziest and dirtiest people in all of Europe if not the entire world. Irishmen were "the sons and daughters of generations of beggars. You can trace the descent in their blighted, stunted forms—in their brassy, cunning, bru-talized features." *Ibid.* The racist Social-Darwinist stereotypes remain the same through the ages.

37. As it is not to this very day. Worse, mass killings of *civilians,* through "area bombings," since World War II have become part of cus-tomary international law.

38. I refer, of course, to the failure of the League of Nations experi-ment in the interwar period.

39. And even this not without risk. See the numerous cases of per-sons dismissed from their jobs or otherwise persecuted and harassed for having been courageous enough to reveal government criminality or corruption.

40. See *New York Times,* March 12, 1976, "Excerpts from Nixon's Responses to the Senate Select Committee on Intelligence."

41. Assassination of Austrian Chancellor Dollfuss, of King Alexander of Yugoslavia, and of French Foreign Minister Louis Barthou, all in 1934.

3.

Ideology and Japanese Foreign Policy
Arthur E. Tiedemann

Let me begin by saying that I intend to use the word ideology in a very limited way. For the purposes of this paper I would roughly define an ideology as a system of ideas concerning relations that exist among states. This system may be regarded as describing these relations *sub specie aeternitatis,* or as revealing a new kind of relation that has been brought into existence by some inevitable historical development, or as presenting the relations that, by some normative concept, ought to exist. Such an ideology can be used as a guide to actions in the international arena. It can also be employed as an argument to justify those actions and to secure the acquiescence or even the participation of others. In this paper I propose to outline briefly some of the more important systems of ideas about state relations that were current in Japan between 1868 and 1945, especially those that have found expression in government policy. My discussion will be confined to ideology as I have defined it, and I will not be examining many other important determinants of foreign policy such as security concerns, economic interests, and so forth. Moreover, I will probe neither to what extent these ideas were really believed by the Japanese nor to what extent they were merely rationalizations. In this respect I would say, however, that my feeling is that ideologies were largely instrumental for the Japanese, and it is difficult to find instances of diplomatic negotiations in which the Japanese government sacrificed a material national interest to achieve some object rooted in an ideological commitment.

Foreigners walking the streets of Tokyo in the late nineteenth century used to be highly amused by what they considered the incongruities in the garments of the Japanese they observed. It was not unusual, for instance, to see a Japanese gentleman dressed in a formal kimono but wearing a derby hat and carrying a furled English umbrella. This mixing of the traditional and the imported is also to be found in Japanese ideologies. Just as scholars have discovered duality in the Japanese economy and in Japanese diplomacy, so it would not be unfair to say that in Japan ideology expressed itself in two styles: one using the traditional terms of the native culture and the other using concepts adapted from the West. I should like first to discuss the traditional ideology, for I believe that with respect to some very crucial points it had a fundamental effect upon Japanese attitudes in the conduct of their foreign relations.

In 1868, when the new and shaky Meiji government undertook to build a modern unified nation, it was confronted with a land characterized by highly particularistic local loyalties. The emperor was the one symbol with the potential for fostering a new national loyalty and for legitimizing the development of a highly centralized state. In turn the legitimation of the emperor's position depended upon Japan's Shinto traditions, and the Meiji government therefore elevated Shinto beliefs and ceremonies into a state cult that was assiduously propagated through history and morals lessons in all Japanese schools and through mass participation in rituals at state-supported Shinto shrines. Throughout the prewar period no effort was spared in using government agencies and other media of mass communications to indoctrinate every

Japanese in the tenets of State Shinto.[1]

Among the articles of faith propounded by State Shinto were: 1. The emperor is the blood-descendent of the Sun Goddess, the living extension in time of the Sun Goddess, and is owed unquestioned loyalty and obedience; 2. The ancestral deities who produced Japan and the rest of the world extend special guardianship to Japan and the Japanese; 3. All Japanese are descendents of the gods and form a blood-family of which the emperor is the father-ruler; 4. Each Japanese is by nature good and will intuitively do the proper thing, if only his intuition is not impaired by the presence of foreign ideas; 5. The Japanese state, the *kokutai,* was designed by the gods, so it and its institutions are unchangeable and are the most excellent state structure in the world; 6. Japanese can find their fulfillment in serving the state and in merging their personal destinies into the greater destiny of the nation; 7. The imperial line has been commissioned by its ancestral gods to share the blessings of Japan's matchless institutions with less fortunate lands, and therefore the emperor's rule "shall be extended so as to embrace all the six quarters and the whole world shall be brought under one roof."[2]

The last proposition, of course, is the most interesting from the point of view of international relations. In Japanese it is known as the *hakkō ichiu* doctrine, "the universe under one roof," and I would like to elucidate it further with D.C. Holtom's paraphrase of an exposition to be found in one of the widely used teacher's commentaries:

> The phrase "the whole world under one roof" does not mean bald aggression and military exploitation, as those affected by the materialism and individualism of Europe and America might easily misunderstand it to mean. It means the establishment in the earth of peace and right-eousness, aiming to cover the whole world with the illuminating rays of charity, love, virtue, truth and justice. When each nation and race has opportunity to fulfil its rightful

destiny, take its place in the sun, express its will and own
special characteristics of culture and racial soul, and thus
make its unique contribution to the general good, then the
doctrine will be realized. All the peoples of the world, with
mutual assistance and good will, will then live together as
one great family. At the same time the leadership of Japan
in this benevolent reconstruction of the world must be
recognized. The *hakkō ichiu* teaching involves the purpose
to extend to the four seas the imperial glory which now fills
Japan herself and thereby bring in the universal reign of
peace. This in turn involves the use of military power, but
history shows that the military might of Japan is always
that of a "divine soldiery that is sent to bring life to all
things."[3]

The *hakkō ichiu* doctrine was a favorite of the military, and
the following quotation with reference to it from an army
minister's speech in 1916 is typical: "Since the foundation of
the Japanese Empire it has been the yearning of all Japanese
to unite all the races of the world into a happy society. We
regard this as the great mission of the Japanese people. We
strive also to clear away from the earth injustice and inequali-
ty and to bring everlasting happiness to mankind."[4]

For the weak Japan of the late nineteenth century Shinto
ideals were strictly for domestic use and did not become the
goals of foreign policy. The operative ideology was Social
Darwinism, a theory that the Japanese had learned from
Herbert Spencer and that they felt was confirmed by their
experience with the activities of the Western powers in Asia
and other parts of the globe. Speaking to a young idealist
around 1885, a prominent Japanese statesman said:

What kind of world do you think this is? It's a world in
which strong countries annex weak countries, develop them
and make them serve their purposes, and fight over them.
To live in a world of struggle like this, we have to build up
our military strength. Nobody without military power can
stand in a world like this. No matter how civilized Korea

became, do you think that the powers that grab what they
want like ravenous wolves would let up? . . . The only way
for Japan to preserve its independence for the long future is
to acquire territory on the mainland. The only territory it
can get on the mainland is in Korea and China. You students spout all kinds of nonsensical teachings about justice. . . . The scholars limit themselves to windy . . . arguments about the way Western countries should stop their
aggression and fighting. But it's different with responsible
political leaders like us. To wage war in order to make one's
country strong is the highest justice and [the highest] loyalty to country and ruler.[5]

In this ruthless world of eat or be eaten, a nation proved it
had the necessary vigor to survive by ceaselessly expanding.
Because the Japanese were determined to survive, expansion
became a dominant motif in modern Japan. As Akira Iriye,
probably the foremost historian of U.S.-Japanese relations,
has noted, "expansion whether by force or through peaceful
methods, whether of Japanese goods, capital, or ideas, whether by colonization or emigration was a perceived necessity
which never left Japanese consciousness after the Meiji Restoration."[6] This expansion included peaceful activities such as
emigration to Hawaii and the U.S. Pacific Coast, but also
prominent was the idea that to secure its own independence
and achieve equality with the world powers, Japan must participate in imperialism. "Let us," said the Japanese foreign
minister in 1887, "convert our country into a European-style
empire. Let us change our people into a European-style people. Let us create in the Orient a new empire on the European model."[7] The Sino-Japanese War of 1894-1895 moved
Japan well along the path of accomplishing this goal and was
also a demonstration of its success in mastering Western tech-
niques and modernizing. The war against China was spoken
of as a struggle "between a country which is trying to advance civilization and a country which disturbs the development of civilization,"[8] as a "clash between new European

culture and old East Asian culture."[9] Intoxicated with the
victory of energetic Japan over a slothful China that could
not muster the will to modernize, many Japanese responded
affirmatively to the conclusion drawn by a noted publicist,
Tokutomi Sohō, who claimed that in East Asia only the Japanese understood the nation state and had the political ability
to operate one. "Upon careful consideration of the destiny of
the empire of greater Japan," he wrote, "I realize that it
bears a special mission. What is that mission? To spread the
benefits of its political organization throughout [East Asia
and Southeast Asia]. If we make comparisons with the past,
isn't Japan's mission in modern history the same as Rome's
mission in ancient history?"[10]

By the end of the nineteenth century the Japanese had
dichotomized the world into, on the one hand, the progressive nations that were carrying forward the march of universal civilization and, on the other hand, the backward nations
that were to be brought into the circle of civilization through
the tutelage and control provided by imperialism. Themselves
they included among the progressive nations that shared the
task of imposing order, stability, and civilization. To make
sure that there was no mistake about which group they belonged to, they carefully distanced themselves from their
Asian neighbors, for as one prominent Japanese intellectual
put it, "Those who keep bad company can never escape a bad
reputation."[11]

Around the time of the Russo-Japanese War, the Japanese
began to wonder if that dichotomy had been the correct one.
Western publicists continually spoke of Western civilization
rather than a universal civilization and seemed to believe that
there was a racial test for participation in it. The Kaiser was
agitating about the Yellow Peril and Admiral Mahan had proclaimed that the West stood "at the opening of a period when
the question is to be settled decisively . . . whether Eastern
or Western civilization is to dominate throughout the earth

and to control its future."[1][2] Although newly imposed racial exclusion policies barred Japanese access to many parts of the world and thus restricted their activity to East Asia, Americans were beginning to oppose the Japanese even in China, and not simply as one imperial power competing with another but on the high moral ground that the struggle was over "whether the institutions and ethical standards of East or West shall shape the course of civilization there."[1][3] America was not only challenging the predominant role in China that Japan felt to be a natural right but was doing it on what appeared to be racial grounds. In these new circumstances many Japanese leaders became concerned about the "White Peril" and began to express fear of a racial war.[1][4] The question arose as to whether the real dichotomy was not between East and West, and that therefore Japan's destiny was not cooperation with the Western imperialist nations, but rather the use of its power to lead an Asian resistance to the West. This kind of perception was encouraged by the enthusiastic response of Asian colonial peoples to Japan's victory over Russia.

The Terauchi Cabinet, which came to power in 1916, was dominated by men who subscribed to this line of thought and who felt that the primary aim of their policy toward China should be to develop the solidarity of the yellow race in preparation for the coming global struggle between the races.[1][5] At a time when Confucianism was being discredited in China they cast their approach in terms of the old Confucian ideals. Japan, they claimed, had abandoned the exploitative practices of the West and was now following the kingly way *(wang tao)*, the way of the ruler who governed by moral example, as opposed to the despot's way *(pa tao)*, the way of the ruler who imposed his will by brute force. Through loans and blandishments they sought to induce the Chinese leaders to cooperate economically with Japan and set up what they called an oriental autarkic sphere. The arguments of one apologist for this policy ran as follows: Japan and China were inseparably bound in one huge family by common racial, geographical, cultural, political, economic, and military bonds.[16] Japan's sole objective was to guarantee the survival of the united yellow race. Japan's actions in China might seem, it was argued, superficially similar to those of the Western powers, but in character they really differed because China's true interests were identical with Japan's and therefore nothing Japan did could possibly harm China. Japan had to be strong in order to protect China from the predatory West and ensure China's integrity and development. Consequently, China should accept the Japanese presence in China as part of the contribution China must make to a joint Japanese-Chinese endeavor to drive out the West and maintain China's integrity.

The policies of the Terauchi Cabinet had little success in China and were bitterly opposed by the majority of Japan's Foreign Ministry personnel, who felt that the old concepts of international relations were still valid. When the Terauchi Cabinet left office at the end of World War I, the next cabinet returned to the policy of cooperation with the Western powers and subscribed to the new world political and economic order established by the Versailles Treaty and the Washington Conference treaties.

There were, of course, Japanese who were dissatisfied with the new world order. As early as 1918 Prince Konoe Fumimaro, a member of the Versailles delegation and prime minister in the late 1930s, protested that the proposed Versailles settlement subordinated Japan to the West and was an attempt to freeze into permanence a situation that was highly favorable to the United States and England.[17] It did not represent a universal morality and did not do justice to Japan's security and economic interests. It would block the expansion necessary for Japan to achieve self-sufficiency and independence.

Around the same time a right-wing ultranationalist, Kita Ikki, was writing a book on the reconstruction of Japanese political life that was to become very influential with young military officers. In that book he urged a foreign policy based on what he called the "Revolutionary Greater Japanese Empire." Just as there is a class struggle within a country, he argued, so there is an international proletarian war between the "have not" countries and the "have" countries, and distributive justice on the international scene is effected by the sword. "England," he wrote, "is a multimillionaire standing over the whole world. Russia is the great landlord of the northern hemisphere. Japan is in the position of an international proletarian with a string of small islands for boundaries. Does Japan not have the right to go to war and seize their monopolies in the name of justice?"[18] Yes, he answered, and calculated that in the near future Japan's growing population would justify the acquisition of Australia, New Zealand, and the Russian Far East. Japan also had the right, he held, to go to war on behalf of another state or people oppressed by unjust force (e.g., China or India), and he urged that his reconstructed Japan become the leader of an Asian confederacy that would liberate Asia.

The ideas of Kita Ikki were symptomatic of an uneasiness in Japan about the Versailles-Washington Conference concept of world order, an uneasiness that was to become deeper and more widespread as the 1920s drew on. Japan's economic position in China had stagnated, and what advantages the nation possessed were being threatened by Chinese nationalism; rising tariff barriers were hampering her trade with the Western world and its colonies; the return of Russian power to the Far East aroused anxiety about military security. To many Japanese it seemed that their nation was economically dependent on the West and that this economic dependence was being exploited to prevent Japan from taking the steps her interests required. People were casting around for a new vision of the world that would chart an independent path for Japan, and one of the most persuasive and influential theories came from a young army officer, Ishiwara Kanji.[19] As an instructor at the Army Staff College, Ishiwara was able to spread his thought among officers destined for important commands. As operations officer of the Kwantung Army, he took the first step toward the implementation of his ideas by playing the chief role in the staging of the Manchurian Incident of 1931. Later, as chief of operations for the Army General Staff, he formulated the plans for Japan's conversion into a "national defense state."

Ishiwara's system of ideas was an ingenious combination of Buddhist eschatology, Shinto beliefs, Social Darwinism, and military history. His Buddhist elements he drew from the Nichiren sect, a highly nationalistic group that identified service to Buddhism with service to the Japanese state and had no compunction about using the sword in the cause of "righteousness." Nichiren Buddhism taught that the world was steadily degenerating through successive stages of increasing violence toward a final cataclysmic end. After the destruction, there would be a new age of eternal peace in which a Japanese Buddhist state would become the Holy See of a new universal religion. Japan would achieve this destiny because it was the home of the gods and possessed in its *kokutai* the supreme moral principles handed down through its unbroken line of emperors. To which Ishiwara added the idea that "the Japanese armed forces are the guardian deity of that righteousness—the Japanese *kokutai*—which shall save the world."[20] Basing his calculations on Buddhist eschatology, Ishiwara predicted that the coming Armageddon would occur around 1970. This date was confirmed, he believed, by his studies in military history. By 1970 the development of military weapons would have reached the point where a truly decisive world war could be fought, e.g., there would be bombers that could circle the globe without landing, and the power of these weapons would be so devastating that no further war would be possible. Mankind would have fought its "Final War." The two protagonists in that clash would be Japan and the United States.

The final titanic war between Japan and the United States would be, Ishiwara said, "the product of divine will, the great natural tide of human civilization."[21] All history had been a continual struggle among human societies for the survival of the fittest, and that struggle had led to higher and higher levels of human culture. War is "the mother of civilizations." Each nation had the duty "to participate in this process, to develop its own ideal, . . . to proclaim it to other nations and through it to seek to guide the destiny of the world."[22] In the West, nations had competed with inherently selfish motives and had followed the "despot's way." From that competition the United States was emerging as the power center embodying Western values. In Asia, where the "kingly way" had been the mode of competition, Japan had become the leader, not through war but rather because its many centuries of energetic cultural borrowing and assimilation had produced the most inclusive cultural synthesis of any nation in history. In the "Final War" Japan must be the victor "for the sake of . . . the salvation of the world."[23] Out of the holocaust would come "a golden age of human culture, a synthesis of East and West, the last and highest stage of human civilization."[24] Japan's "powerful enemies will be vanquished, the glorious spirit of the Japanese *kokutai* will come home to the hearts of the peoples of all nations, and the world will enter an era of peace under the guidance of the imperial throne."[25]

As a first step toward securing the resources necessary to fight the decisive war with America and to discharge Japan's holy mission, Ishiwara asserted that Japan had the moral right to seize control of Manchuria. By this step Japan would not only gain a resource base but in that multiracial area the

Japanese would be able to build an ideal state that would be a model of racial harmony and mutual profit. Japan would bring order, stability, and prosperity to Manchuria, a task of which the Chinese were incapable because they had no political capacity and could not construct a modern state. There would be racial equality, but the Japanese would direct the new country because "their natural talents as a modern race and their great mission as the liberators and unifiers of Asia not only justified a position of leadership . . . but also insured that they would act selflessly for the good of all races."[26] Equality for the other races would consist in their being given positions and tasks appropriate to their inherent levels of ability. Success in Manchuria should lead to the same type of cooperation in China Proper, but if the Chinese did not see that it was in their own interests to support Japan in the struggle to liberate Asia, then Japan should not hesitate to use sheer force to coerce them into working for their own true good.

As mentioned earlier, Ishiwara Kanji was a man of action as well as a theorist. He did actually engineer the seizure of Manchuria and thus began the long series of events that ultimately culminated in the Greater East Asian Co-Prosperity Sphere and the Pacific War. However, although Japanese leaders were willing to embrace Ishiwara's plan of action, most of them did so without accepting the theory behind it. His ideas, while arousing chords of response among the Japanese, were too idiosyncratic, too parochial, too bound up with a particular religious view. For the acceptance of their case by the world community, by the Asian community, and even by the more sophisticated of the Japanese community, the need was felt for the assertion of more generally accepted norms than the tenets of Nichiren Buddhism and Shinto. For reasons rooted deeply in their cultural history, the Japanese are given to seeking for signs of the direction in which the times are moving and then using their perception of what they conceive to be the inevitable trend of events as a basis for planning actions that will take proper advantage of the ineluctable movement of history. Even though in the 1930s the Japanese wanted to depart from the Versailles-Washington Conference order and strike out on an independent path defined by themselves strictly in terms of their own needs, there was still a desire to feel that they were part of a universal trend and in modern Japanese history universal trends have frequently been interpreted as what the Westerners were doing.

Observing the Ottawa system of imperial preferences and the Pan-American activities of the United States, Japanese drew the lesson in the early 1930s that the world was breaking up into economic blocs.[27] Consequently, they advanced the argument that all they were trying to do in East Asia was to establish a Japanese version of the Monroe Doctrine. However, as the 1930s advanced and the Nazis began to elaborate their conception of a new order in Europe, Japanese theorists began to perceive the Monroe Doctrine as only a particular example of a trend with much greater universal significance. Cultural heritage, racial ties, and geography, they held, divided the world into a number of great regions, and the present stage of world technology and economics required organization into such large areas. The old concept of a universally applicable international law had to be replaced by the concept of differing regional law systems based on the particular situation of each region. In the existing state of world development the leading state within each region had the moral right to insist that all the peoples of the region sublimate their nationalist feeling into a regional loyalty and join in a regional structure that would provide for their common security and prosperity. The region's leading state also had the obligation of determining what goals were essential for the common good and welfare of the entire region. To achieve these goals they would establish a hierarchy of peoples and assign each people a role appropriate in terms of that people's intrinsic capacities. Naturally, the leading state would be responsible for maintaining the stability of the region and for preventing outsiders from intruding into the region. Eventually there would emerge a fixed number of such great regions that would be so equally matched in military and economic power that no one region could threaten the security of another, and thus there would be a new peaceful world order.

In East Asia, the theorists argued, Japan was trying to create such a regional structure, an entity into whose collective destiny all the peoples of the region would be able to merge their national destinies—as the Americans were doing in the Western Hemisphere, the Italians and Germans were doing in Europe and Africa, and the Russians were doing in Eastern Europe. The successful completion of Japan's righteous task would lead not only to regional peace but would also contribute to the peace of the entire world. The main obstacles to Japan's success were a misguided Chinese nationalism and Anglo-American imperialism, the link between the two being Chiang Kai-shek, who was cooperating with the Western powers. The war against China and, later, the Pacific War were therefore "holy wars" being fought for the highest moral and idealistic purposes.

The themes and moral claims just outlined permeated the Japanese statements issued about the "New Order in East Asia," or the "Greater East Asia Co-Prosperity Sphere," or the Pacific War and are even to be found in their official communications to foreign governments. To the Western powers Japan asserted that it was helping to replace an outmoded world order with a new regional order more consonant with the times; to Asian peoples Japan based its appeal on anticolonialism and race, asking that they accept Japanese direction and subordinate themselves to the great task of driving out the white colonialists, liberating Asia, and establishing a prosperity in which all would share; from her own people Japan demanded the sacrifices required to seize the leadership of East Asia not simply to satisfy economic or security needs but also to further the task laid upon them by the ancient injunction of their ancestral gods and to contribute to the betterment of their fellow Asians and all human kind. Not surprisingly, it was with its own people that Japan had the most success. In the greater East Asian region Japan never did manage to solve its ideological problem, which was to create an ideology that would accord enough political equality and rewards to attract the support of Asians and yet that would justify to those same Asians the reservation of a position of political paramountcy and economic dominance for Japan.

NOTES

1. For a detailed exposition of the connection between State Shinto and Japanese nationalism, see D.C. Holtom, *Modern Japan and Shinto Nationalism*, rev. ed. (Chicago, 1947).

2. Satomi Kishio, *Hakkō Ichiu - Tōa Shinchitsujo to Nihon Kokutai* [Hakkō Ichiu - the new order in East Asia and the Japanese national polity] (Tokyo, 1940), p. 123, gives the original passage in the *Nihon Shoki*, an eighth century chronicle from which this phrase is drawn.

3. Holtom, *op. cit.*, p. 23.

4. *Ibid.*, p. 22.

5. Soejima Taneomi, quoted in Marius B. Jansen, "Japanese Views of China During the Meiji Period," in Albert Feuerwerker, Rhoads Murphey, and Mary C. Wright, eds., *Approaches to Modern Chinese History* (Berkeley, 1967), pp. 171-172.

6. Akira Iriye, "Kayahara Kazan and Japanese Cosmopolitanism," in Albert M. Craig and Donald H. Shively, eds., *Personality in Japanese History* (Berkeley, 1970), p. 397.

7. Inoue Kaoru Denki Hensankai, *Segai Inoue Kō Den* [Life of Marquis Inoue], 5 vols. (Tokyo, 1933-1934), vol. 3:919.

8. Fukuzawa Yūkichi's newspaper, the *Jiji Shimpō*, quoted in Hilary Conroy, *The Japanese Seizure of Korea: 1868-1910* (Philadelphia, 1960), p. 255, slightly modified.

9. Mutsu Munemitsu, Japanese foreign minister in 1894, quoted in Akira Iriye, "Imperialism in East Asia," in James B. Crowley, ed., *Modern East Asia: Essays in Interpretation* (New York, 1970), p. 137.

10. Quoted in Marlene Mayo, *The Emergence of Imperial Japan—Self-Defense or Calculated Aggression* (Boston, 1970), p. 66. This statement appeared in an essay entitled "Romans and Japanese," written in July 1895. That same month Tokutomi wrote an essay on "Barbaric Spirit and Civilized Knowledge" in which he said, "The union of barbaric vigor and civilized learning is the greatest force in the world." See Kenneth B. Pyle, *The New Generation in Meiji Japan - Problems of Cultural Identity, 1885-1895* (Stanford, 1969), p. 181.

11. Fukuzawa Yūkichi, quoted in Sannosuke Matsumoto, "Yūkichi Fukuzawa - His Concept of Civilization and View of Asia," *Developing Economies*, 5:1 (1967):169. This quotation is from Fukuzawa's famous essay "Japan Should Detach Herself from Asia," published in 1885. See also Kimitada Miwa, "Fukuzawa's 'Departure from Asia,'" in Edmund Skrzypczak, ed., *Japan's Modern Century* (Tokyo, 1968), pp. 1-26.

12. Akira Iriye, *Pacific Estrangement - Japanese and American Expansion, 1897-1911* (Cambridge, Mass., 1972), p. 31.

13. *Ibid.*, p. 226.

14. See Peter Duus, "Nagai Ryūtarō and the 'White Peril,' 1905-1944," *Journal of Asian Studies*, 31:1 (1971):41-48. Also for a high-ranking Japanese statesman's premonitions about a racial war see Roger Hackett, *Yamagata Aritomo in the Rise of Modern Japan, 1838-1922* (Cambridge, Mass., 1971), p. 274, as well as Ryusaku Tsunoda, Wm. Theodore de Bary, and Donald Keene, *Sources of the Japanese Tradition* (New York, 1958), pp. 714-716.

15. See Frank C. Langdon, "The Japanese Policy of Expansion in China, 1917-1928" (Ph.D. diss., University of California, Berkeley, 1953), as well as his "Japan's Failure to Establish Friendly Relations with China in 1917-1918," *Pacific Historical Review*, 26 (1957):245-258. See also Akira Iriye, "The Ideology of Japanese Imperialism: Imperial Japan and China," in Grant K. Goodman, comp., *Imperial Japan and Asia - A Reassessment.* Occasional Papers of the East Asian Institute (New York, 1967), pp. 32-45.

16. This apologist was Hanzawa Gyokujō, the editor of the *Gaikō Jihō* [Diplomatic Review], who made these points in a number of pieces written for that journal during the 1920s and the 1930s. Professor Shumpei Okamoto is studying the attitudes of Hanzawa and other Japanese toward China in the 1920s. See his "Japanese Response to Chinese Nationalism: Naitō (Ko'nan) Torajirō's Image of China in the 1920s," in F. Gilbert Chan and Thomas H. Etzold, eds., *China in the*

1920s (New York and London, 1976), pp. 160-175.

17. Gordon M. Berger, "Ajia Shinchitsujo no yume" [A dream of a new Asian order], in Satō Seisaburō and R. Dingman, eds., *Kindai Nihon no Taigai Taidō* [Modern Japanese attitudes toward the outside world] (Tokyo, 1974), pp. 193-194. See also in the same volume, R. Dingman, "Nihon to Wirusonteki Sekai Chitsujo" [Japan and the Wilsonian world order], pp. 93-122. Also see Kimitada Miwa, "Japanese Opinions of Woodrow Wilson in War and Peace," *Monumenta Nipponica*, 22:3/4 (1967):382-383.

18. Kōichi Nomura, "Ikki Kita," *Developing Economies*, 4:4 (1966):241-242. See also George M. Wilson, *Radical Nationalist in Japan: Kita Ikki, 1883-1937* (Cambridge, Mass., 1969), p. 82.

19. Ishiwara's ideas are explored in great detail in Mark R. Peattie, *Ishiwara Kanji and Japan's Confrontation with the West* (Princeton, 1975).

20. *Ibid.*, pp. 54-55.

21. *Ibid.*, p. 57.

22. *Ibid.*, p. 55.

23. *Ibid.*, p. 57.

24. *Ibid.*, p. 58.

25. *Ibid.*, p. 74.

26. *Ibid.*, p. 173.

27. For material on the points made in this and the following two paragraphs see Mitani Taichirō, "Changes in Japan's International Position and the Response of Japanese Intellectuals: Trends in Japanese Studies of Japan's Foreign Relations, 1931-1941," in Dorothy Borg and Shumpei Okamoto, eds., *Pearl Harbor as History - Japanese-American Relations, 1931-1941* (New York, 1973), pp. 575-594; James B. Crowley, "Intellectuals as Visionaries of the New Asian Order," in James W. Morley, ed., *Dilemmas of Growth in Prewar Japan* (Princeton, 1971), pp. 319-373; James B. Crowley, "A New Asian Order: Some Notes on Prewar Japanese Nationalism," in Bernard S. Silberman and H. D. Harootunian, eds., *Japan in Crisis - Essays on Taishō Democracy* (Princeton, 1974), pp. 270-298; James B. Crowley, "A New Deal for Japan and Asia: One Road to Pearl Harbor," in Crowley, *Modern East Asia: Essays in Interpretation*, pp. 235-264; Joyce C. Lebra, *Japan's Greater East Asia Co-Prosperity Sphere in World War II: Selected Readings and Documents* (Kuala Lumpur, 1975); F. C. Jones, *Japan's New Order in East Asia - Its Rise and Fall, 1937-1945* (London, 1954).

4.

The Impact of Ideologies on the Conduct of International Relations
René Albrecht-Carrié

There are those who would claim that the state is an obsolete institution, no longer suited to the world of modern technology. A strong case can be made for such a contention, and the purpose of the following observations is to examine the impact of certain forces, more particularly ideologies of a universalistic character, upon that situation. The restricted meaning of the term ideology that is implied is deliberate lest the discussion broaden into unmanageable dimensions. Although the modern nation state as we know it is itself a fairly recent creation, the situation is not new, but the technology of our day, including weaponry under that rubric, gives the problem an urgency that it has not had in the past.

Leo Tolstoy's *War and Peace* was followed a century later by Raymond Aron's *Peace and War*.[1] Monumental works as they both are, they may seem to have little in common beyond the inverted similarity of their titles. Yet the problem of universal peace is an ancient preoccupation of mankind; within our own century it has twice resulted in the formal establishment of organizations the ostensible purpose of which was the creation of that presumably desirable condition. The adverb is used advisedly, for the contrary view may not be ignored that strife is the law of existence. Indeed it is not difficult to make a case for the contention that, given a suitable definition of the term, war has been an instrument of progress. But the consensus on the desirability of peace has reached overwhelming adherence, at least among those possessed of the most powerful engines of destruction.

Ours is a world of states, and the state, like other living organisms, competes with others of its kind, seeking to aggrandize itself at their expense. The *ultima ratio regum,* war, is the final consequence of this characteristic of the state. The state, in addition, has claimed—still claims—the attribute of sovereignty, a logical consequence of which is that an anarchic condition prevails on the international scene. Yet that anarchy has been qualified by the acknowledgment of common interest, most simply the shared desire for survival.

Hence the acceptance of certain rules, of which two are fundamental: The legitimacy of competition has been acknowledged as one, but so have limitations on the effects of that competition. Thus no one should be totally destroyed, an understanding generally respected although some exceptions to it can be cited.[2] There has even developed a discipline called international law. Impotent reed as it may be in the absence of enforcing power, it has nevertheless given rise to voluminous writing and attracted the efforts of very distinguished minds.

It must be realized that the state of affairs just described is a relatively recent development. The European state system, with its concomitant of power equilibrium, has become extended to the entire world. In recent centuries Europe conquered the planet, taking that word in the broad sense to mean transferring to the rest of the world its ways and institutions, the use of force by the conquerors as well as willing imitation on the part of the conquered being part of the process. The decades since the end of the Second World War have witnessed the termination of the conquering aspect of that process, but those parts of the former European colonial empires that have emerged into independence seem to have been unable to think of solutions other than the emulation of the ways of their former masters, be it in terms of their domestic structures or in their claims to the customary prerogatives of the state, sovereignty not the least among them.[3]

The world system of states has run into difficulties. One of these—there are several—stems from the simple fact of geographical dimensions. Modern technology, under which label the economy must be included, demands for its effective operation units of continental size. From this standpoint the United States, the Soviet Union, and China, to cite a few examples, may be considered adequate. The size of the separate units of Europe, among them the great powers of yesterday, is no longer sufficient; that is one reason for their common demotion, although in union they could achieve major status, and seen in this context the movement for European unity appears as a response to the factor of size. A large number of the units that have become members of the United Nations simply do not make sense, however much one may respect their desire for independence.

Traditionally, the formation of larger units was the result of conquest. That was the story of the formation of a number of the European national states, France, Germany, and others, but the process was checked by the intrusion of the nationalistic virus. The attempts to enforce unity, be they Napoleon's or Hitler's, have come too late, even apart from other considerations that made such attempts, the second especially, totally unacceptable.

But the Roman Empire too was the result of conquest, and this suggests a very relevant consideration. Modern nationalism was unknown to the ancient world, and after the initial use of force, the Roman conquest was willingly accepted. This was especially the case in the less advanced (civilized) west. The Gauls became Romanized with surprising rapidity and ease, after a time almost more Roman than the Romans

themselves; the modern French have sometimes claimed—
with pride—to be the most authentic heirs of the Latin genius, and the ethnic origin of Roman emperors was quite
varied.

As to the Germanic barbarians, even if they eventually
turned out to be the instrument that destroyed Rome, they
had no higher ambition than to become integrated into what
they willingly acknowledged to be a higher stage of development. Indeed they could think of nothing better than trying
to set up that terminological inconsistency, the Holy Roman
Empire of the German Nation.

The very name implied the convergence of divergent
forces, the acceptance, for one thing, of the values for which
Rome had stood, the propriety of the political unity of mankind.[4] The long duration of the Roman Empire, which be-
stowed upon Western mankind the boon of the *Pax Romana,*
made a profound impression on its beneficiaries, and it had
the effect of creating a persistent belief in the desirability of
restoring political unity long after the possibility of reestablishing that condition had vanished. The Christian Church, in
some fundamental respects the true heir of imperial Rome,
adhered to the same faith, bolstered by its emphasis on the
common humanity of man; to this day the Church of Rome
has persisted in denying the validity of distinctions based on
color or race. And indeed how else could it be, for it was a
question of dealing with truth leading to ultimate salvation, a
truth that was assumed to be unique and universal.

The persistence of this outlook was manifested in the institution that was the Holy Roman Empire. This is not the
place to dwell upon the vicissitudes of that creation, the
quarrel between the secular and the religious powers, and the
eventual success of the former, but it is well to remember
that the Holy Roman Empire was not formally abolished
until Napoleon's time, even if one allows that, long before
that, it had become a shell devoid of content.

Seventeenth-century Pascal considered himself a faithful adherent of the Church of Rome. Yet he also delivered himself of the judgment *vérité en deçá des Pyrénées, erreur au delà* (truth on one side of the Pyrenees is error on the other), a trenchant way of expressing the relativity of truth, a point of view to which the awakening of the Renaissance, the Reformation and the religious wars to which it gave rise, then the success of the scientific endeavor, powerfully contributed.

But it is also worth recalling the common ground of the Enlightenment, manifested, among other things, in the civilized manner in which eighteenth-century wars were conducted. The activity of English Captain Cook, a scientific enterprise, was not to be interfered with by the fact that Britain and France were at war with each other. Thus the eighteenth century presents an interesting dichotomy: A world of rival states, or sovereign princes, that professed adherence to and honored certain common values.

No better expression of this common ground can be cited than the thrust of the social thought of the day directed to the proper organization of the Society of Man. Certain aspects of the explosion that occurred in France as the century was drawing to a close are worth considering for their relevance to the present discussion.

Most relevant of all was the universality of the approach of those who came to lead the revolution. That revolution should occur in France was entirely fitting, France being the most advanced state of the Continent and the seat of the capital of European culture. The enactments that issued from Versailles, then from Paris, were of equal applicability in other quarters, a fact that found expression in the welcome given initially by many to the armies of the Revolution, seen as liberators rather than conquerors, along the Rhine and across the Alps. And we may recall the decree, issued by the

Convention on 19 November 1792, that stated that "the National Convention declares that it will grant assistance and fraternity to all peoples who wish to recover their liberty," as well as the fact that the *Marseillaise* was adopted by the Second International as its anthem.

But the word initially is important, for it is intimately related to the dichotomy—or inconsistency—that characterized the eighteenth-century condition.

The central issue of the French Revolution was a shift in the basis of the legitimacy of state power from the monarch to the nation, or the people, in broad terms the introduction of the concept of democracy.[5] This shift had ambivalent effects, for putting the people at the center of the source of state power could result in democracy but it also contained the seed of national self-determination. The French deserve much credit—or blame—for launching modern nationalism on its subsequently disastrous course.

Hence the confusion that ensued and that the Napoleonic wars illustrate to perfection. Napoleon himself ever claimed that he was a son of the Revolution and even professed a desire to establish unity in Europe. The validity of these contentions must be set against the fact that the revolutionary ideology could also be seen as no more than a novel tool in the armory of French power.

It may be worth stopping a moment to give a striking illustration of this second aspect of the matter. It occurred a quarter of a century after Napoleon's final defeat and the ostensible Viennese restoration of the old order. Britain and France, traditional imperial rivals, found themselves involved in 1840 in a confrontation arising from their competing interests in the Near East. France was supporting the attempt of the Egyptian ruler, Mohammed Ali, technically a vassal of the Turkish Sultan, to establish himself in independence while simultaneously enlarging his domain. Britain, fearing the establishment of a French base in Egypt, favored the preservation of the integrity of the Ottoman Empire. War between the Sultan and his vassal was at one remove an Anglo-French clash, a preview in some of its aspects of the Greco-Turkish clash of the nineteen twenties. In 1840 there was danger that the war between the clients might escalate into a direct confrontation between their respective patrons.

The bourgeois French king, Louis Philippe, had no inclination for war. Adolphe Thiers, his chief minister, always favored an Anglo-French alliance, but in this particular instance he misjudged the possibilities of a show of intransigence. As the danger of war seemed to grow he was dismissed, to be replaced by the less flamboyant and also anglophile Guizot. But Guizot too was in charge of the French interest, and it is revealing to quote his appraisal of the prospects of the situation:

> Should France go to war in order that the Pasha of Egypt keep Syria?
> Obviously, this is not a sufficiently large interest to become a cause of war. France, which did not go to war to liberate Poland from Russia and Italy from Austria, cannot reasonably do so in order that Syria should be in the hands of the Pasha rather than those of the Sultan.
> The war would be either oriental and naval, or continental and general. If naval, the disparity of forces, damage, and risks is undeniable. *If continental and general, France could only sustain it by giving it a revolutionary character,* . . .[6]

Of conservative inclination himself, hence excluding the possibility of a revolutionary war, and therefore compelled to fall back on a measured and realistic appraisal of the concrete facts of power, Guizot wisely opted for yielding. But what is of interest, and the reason for citing the episode, is the fact that he was fully aware of other possibilities, *the exploitation of the ideological factor as a compensatory substitute for the material deficiencies of French power.* That the awareness

was justified, that the possibility existed, is shown by the
Europe-wide revolutionary outbreaks that shook much of the
Continent eight years later on the heels of the Parisian initiative and of which it has been said that by her failure to assist
other revolutionary movements France saved the peace at the
price of killing the revolution.

During the course of the nineteenth century the democratic seed planted in 1789 greatly prospered. The revolutions of 1830 and 1848 in France, then the aftermath of the
Franco-Prussian War in the form of the Third Republic, following the interlude of the Second Empire, constitute a
steady extension of the democratic practice. Avoiding the
stress and discontinuity of revolutions, altered regimes, and
repeated exercises in constitution making, Britain went
through a comparable experience, a fact of which the steady
extension of the franchise was the clearest expression.

The same trend seemed to prevail everywhere, until even in
autocratic Russia, following the defeat by Japan and the
troubles of 1905, the tsar allowed the introduction of a
measure of representative institutions. Democracy seemed to
be the inescapable wave of the future to those living during
the opening decades of the twentieth century, a wave the
progress of which seemed to be accelerated by the First
World War. Nothing could have been more appropriate than
that the slogan "to make the world safe for democracy"
should have been coined by the American president, and the
spate of democratic constitutions with which the defeated
and the new states that emerged from the war proceeded to
endow themselves was more grist to the same mill.

But here two qualifying observations are necessary. The
point has been made that another facet of the democratic
principle may be labeled self-determination. From the simple
fact that a group of individuals is conscious of ethnic affinity—

language is the clearest although not the only or indispensable basis of distinction—it is an easy step to claim the right of distinct political existence. Why should whites lord it over blacks, or Germans over Poles? That the blacks or the Poles might in some ways fare better under such dispensations has come to be regarded as a totally irrelevant consideration, and thus it came to pass that the French Revolution gave an enormous boost to the nationalistic tendency, the progress of which, like that of the franchise, constitutes so large a part of the nineteenth-century story. In this one may see a manifestation of the inconsistency between the universalistic aspect of the democratic force and the narrower, not to say often petty, demands of self-determination.

Yet might not the divergence be brought into harmony? Let indeed the right of self-determination be granted to all, then having received the supposed benefits of that boon, let them all join in free association for the purpose of maintaining international order, world peace. The concept was not new, Mazzini could be credited with it, but it was again appropriate that its sponsorship should be an American contribution. One state, by far the most powerful in the world at the time, through the endeavors of its president, procured the insertion of the Covenant of the League of Nations into the treaties of peace that were drawn up after the First World War.

But in order to obtain this result a dodge, or a flaw, had to be resorted to. The League, whose main function was the preservation of peace, emerged as an association of sovereigns and was not endowed with automatic law-enforcing powers. There is a supreme irony in the fact that the ratification of the Treaty of Versailles by the American Senate foundered on the rock of sovereignty. Whether the League could have been a success had the American decision been otherwise must remain a speculative question, and for our purposes all that need be retained is the failure of the Wilsonian attempt.

Now for the second qualification. There are those who would argue that as the eighteenth passed into the nineteenth century, a more important contribution to the transformation of society than the Enlightenment-generated French Revolution was the primarily English-initiated phenomenon that was the Industrial Revolution. However that may be, there is no denying that much of the debate about individual rights remains an empty and abstract exercise if divorced from a consideration of the economic base. Bourgeois capitalism certainly prospered during the nineteenth century, providing the wherewithal for the improvement of the material conditions of existence, for all that the process was accompanied by the abuses of unfettered property rights and free enterprise.

Criticisms of the system appeared as a result, among which that of Karl Marx has been the most telling. Leaving aside considerations of morality or of the validity of analysis, what matters here is the fact that Marx's views can be seen as a response to certain novel circumstances, most simply the emergence of industry. The economic interpretation of history, the class struggle, like the thought of the Enlightenment or that of Adam Smith, represented ideas that were not confined to the boundaries of a state, their applicability having equal validity everywhere and for all. Like democracy, socialism made progress with the passage of time and the growth of that product of industry that is the industrial proletariat.[7] And, quite properly, socialism was supranational, antinational in fact, in so far as the existing state was seen as a tool in the hands of the ruling capitalist class. The pre-1914 state establishments were much concerned about the possible effects of conscription in the event of war: What direction would the guns take in the hands of the workers who would inevitably constitute a large part of national armies? And meanwhile pre-1914 socialists argued among themselves whether the new society would eventually come into existence through the operation of the democratic franchise or whether violent action would at some point become necessary.

We know what happened. The outbreak of war in 1914 wrecked the Second International, when socialists in the initial belligerent countries found reasons for giving priority to their respective national allegiances. But it is also the unforeseen vicissitudes of the war that brought Lenin to power in Russia. Good Marxist that he was, Lenin had no special interest in Russia *qua* Russia; he was satisfied with exploiting the circumstances and using Russia as a base for the larger purpose of world revolution. Quite properly and consistently, the Bolsheviks appealed to all to follow the Russian example.

But a complicating distortion ensued from the fact of the Russian condition of economic and political backwardness. According to the Marxist book itself, the ultimate proletarian takeover, a stage in a historic process, should have taken place in an advanced industrially developed country, in Russia last of all. The consequence was an inversion of the supposedly proper sequence of development: *Instead of the revolution being the product of industry, the latter would have to be created in Russia by the former.* In the course of time it was, but in the interval there was no alternative to the coercion of the politically uneducated mass; the election of November 1918, having failed to produce a Bolshevik majority, was simply disregarded. Russia has since been operating as a totalitarian dictatorship, a fact that in turn has had incalculable repercussions.

In the last analysis communism is not supposed to be antidemocratic but the opposite, in fact, claiming as it does to be dedicated to the establishment of the good and just society in which man will no longer be exploited by man, incidentally making possible for that reason the ultimate withering of the state. If there was no significant response to the Bolshevik call for world revolution,[8] the appeal of the familiar Marxist doctrine, bolstered and enhanced by the success of revolution in Russia, was considerable. It was quite understandably a source of concern to the ruling establishments of the capitalist states, the reason for their interventions.

Thus the situation *at the end of the First World War* was one in which *two rival ideologies, the democratic and the Marxist, were contending for the allegiance of all.* But the question could also be raised whether the appeal to make the world safe for democracy and the call for world revolution were necessarily incompatible or whether their ultimate aims did not contain sufficient common ground to make a synthesis between them possible. A perusal of Point VI of the Wilsonian Fourteen Points, the one that dealt with the Russian situation, makes interesting rereading.

Again we know what happened. Insofar as the emphasis came to be on capitalism versus communism, enmity and reciprocal suspicion prevailed, but a parallel can also be found between the subsequent impact of the Russian Revolution and that of the earlier French. Let us consider this in some greater detail.

Once it became established that the one point of immediate agreement between the rival systems, the impossibility of their coexistence, was denied by the facts, a de facto stabilization had to occur. War, foreign and civil, had reduced Russia to a condition of chaotic misery which made necessary an enormous task of physical reconstruction. Given her resources and dimensions, Russia, after a while under the guidance of Stalin, opted for the policy of socialism in one country, minimizing, for a time at least, the stress on world revolution.[9] The rest of the world meanwhile limped through the twenty-year interval of the long armistice during which the Great Depression occurred.

It was only an armistice, for the war had left too much

unfinished business. The war had sufficiently injured the pre-existing international structure to make unsuccessful the attempts to restore that structure that were the settlements made after the end of the conflict; hence another breakdown and another world conflict that, from one point of view, essentially completed the work of the first. The world's difficulties have not been settled as a consequence of the Second World War, but the world has been operating since its conclusion in a totally different context from that which had prevailed before the earlier conflict.

From the Second World War the former great powers of Europe save one emerged in a state of common demotion—the club of the defeated—from which, despite their remarkable economic recovery, it is difficult to conceive that they individually will recover their former positions of influence. The Soviet Union is the one exception, for the Soviet state did not collapse but instead, despite fantastic hurt, emerged from the ordeal as a superpower. There was one other superpower, the United States, at war's end uninjured and considerably stronger than the Soviet Union.

As the Second World War was drawing to a close both countries may be said to have picked up the threads where they had left them a quarter of a century before. The United States renounced isolation and embarked instead, with perhaps uncritical enthusiasm, upon the attempt to make the rest of the world in its own image, once more to make it safe for democracy. It was hampered in this endeavor by the contradiction inherent in any attempt to impose freedom by force. But one thing it could do, and that was to support the cry for independence wherever it arose, self-determination unlimited. The demand for emancipation was strong among the subject peoples, the two world wars having given it a great fillip. The result was the destruction of all the European empires, again save one.[10] In their place a multitude of independent states made their appearance on the world map.

The outcome has not necessarily been of the best, rather it has been bizarre in some of its manifestations. Picking up again another Wilsonian idea, the United States, more than any other state, was responsible for the creation of the United Nations, successor to the defunct League, and like the League dedicated above all to the preservation of world peace. From its initial membership of 45 the United Nations had proliferated to more than three times that number, and the end is not yet in sight. In deference to the democratic principle of the equality of states, the members of the United Nations are all sovereign entities, one incidental consequence of this being the irrelevance and the futility of much of the General Assembly's activity.[11] Newcomers to independence, these states have been inordinately jealous of the attribute of sovereignty, and, despite the artificiality that many of them reflect, the result of the arbitrary administrative arrangements of the former colonial powers, they have only too successfully adopted that other European export that nationalism has been. That virus is now more actively at work in their midst than in its native European home.

Marxism claims to be anti-imperialist and, as might be expected, the Soviet Union enthusiastically supported the destruction of the colonial empires. Where the Soviet Union itself was concerned, its continued existence—it was in effect essentially coextensive with the former empire of the tsars—could be justified on the basis of voluntary association. The Second World War had the effect of making it possible for Russia to recover most of the territorial losses suffered in the earlier conflict[12] and, in addition, to extend the effective range of Muscovite control deep into mid-Europe. By 1948 subservient puppet regimes had been established in the countries where the Red Army was present. The earlier prospect of world revolution could be revived through a simple revision of the timetable.

There was in fact an uneasy passage in the western

countries of Europe immediately after the war, when the miserable state of their economies, in combination with the large role played by Communists in the wartime resistance movements, had the effect of giving rise to large Communist parties that even participated in governments. But by 1948 that condition had changed. The strength of the Communist vote remained fairly constant in France and in Italy—one-quarter to one-third of the electorate—but in 1947 the Communist ministers were evicted from their posts in both countries. This was in part the result of domestic opposition, but the American influence had also been at work.

Gone were the days when Franklin D. Roosevelt thought that he could manage Stalin. His successor took a much less conciliatory stand and even startled Molotov by his forthright bluntness; the Truman Doctrine and the Marshall Plan constituted a return to the post-First World War policy of the *cordon sanitaire,* now dubbed containment.[13] But again an ambiguity arose: Was the Soviet-American clash a classical instance of power rivalry, or was it the confrontation of contending ideologies? Actually it was both, the ideological component being increasingly annexed to the purposes of state power. The contention is that in the ideological contest both the United States and the Soviet Union have failed.

Where America was concerned much was made of the threat of Communist ideology and its adjunct, world revolution. The Communist success in China in 1949 was regarded as representing an extension of the domain of Russian control, hence of Russian power. The witch hunt that was the McCarthy episode illustrates the mood that prevailed for a time. Thus, by gradual steps, the United States found itself sucked into a policy of opposing the spread of communism everywhere. The consequences were at times odd, for they meant the support of some highly undemocratic regimes, the American role in the Korean War, and eventually the disastrous involvement in Vietnam.[14] It was awkward indeed for anti-imperialist America to have become the Imperial Republic[15] and to find itself extensively berated as the great imperialistic power of the day. What did America really stand for?

Rather less was heard about Soviet imperialism, for the reason that the appeal of the Marxist doctrine, insofar as it can claim to stand for the redress of the grievances of the oppressed, remains considerable. That simple claim, rather than the subtleties of the economic interpretation of history, is what still moves great masses, with the consequence that, in the free world, large numbers adhere to the doctrine of their own choice.[16]

But that is only part of the story. There was in Europe one country where the Communist dispensation prevailed without the presence of the Red Army. Marshal Tito was undoubtedly an authentic Communist, but he was also a nationalistic Yugoslav. Stalin was wrong when he thought that a shake of his little finger would suffice to dispose of Tito, who instead managed to survive. The outcome was highly unorthodox but of the highest significance, for national communism is a contradiction of terms, a challenge to orthodoxy comparable to the problem of heresy in the history of the Christian Church.

For that reason the impact of the Yugoslav defiance far exceeded the limited bounds of Yugoslav power. A decade later an even more serious challenge appeared when, around 1960, relations began to sour between Mao's China and the Soviet Union. As is usual in the matter of heresy, rival interpreters threw the book at each other while engaging in controversies that to an outsider seemed fully as relevant as some of those among the early Christians on the nature of the Trinity or those that thrived at the time of the Reformation. More recently still, the talk of Eurocommunism bespeaks a spread of the infection.

Thus we have come to a state of affairs comparable to that which attended the nineteenth-century spread of democracy, when, as pointed out before, *the state managed to survive having absorbed the ideology without altering its fundamental nature.* Similarly it would seem that communism has indeed prospered and extended the range of its control without having had much effect on the international structure of states. The three-cornered relationship among the United States, the Soviet Union, and the People's Republic of China, the reestablishment of Sino-American relations, and American-Soviet detente fit to a nicety the classical diplomacy of power relationships. Such a state of affairs may be out of date in a world of mass technology and nuclear weapons; it seems difficult to contend that it is not the world we have.

The deep forces that are transforming our society, and which may best be lumped together under the technological rubric, have put under great strain the existing international structure of states. The nineteenth century managed to operate successfully under the label of freedom: The steadily extended franchise and free enterprise released energies that, among other things, made possible an enormous improvement in the material lot of those who lived in the technologically developed world. But they also contained the seeds of possible destruction, and the framework is cracking at the seams.

As indicated before, modern technology needs for its effective operation geographical units of continental dimensions. The United States, the Soviet Union, and China make sense from this standpoint; Chad, not to mention Anguilla, does not. Even the former great powers of Western Europe have been trying to organize collectively to assert a position. The result for the moment has been a return to an international structure similar to the nineteenth-century European, the cast of participants being new but the same rules of the game of power relationships prevailing. The possibility, the inescapability some would say, of world organization, not to mention world government, has not been realized, *for the universalistic ideologies of democracy and communism have both failed to overcome divergence,* and it is too early to tell whether the multinational corporation may produce an alternative organization that may provide the possibility of adaptation to conditions with which the national territorial state seems no longer capable of dealing.

The existing shape of the international structure is patently inadequate to the needs of the day, be it from the standpoint of effective economic operations or from that of preserving the peace, both overriding necessities. In the process of evolving toward another type that is capable of meeting those needs, *the intrusion of ideologies has so far had a confusing and complicating effect.* What has been said so far has shown the contortions, the inconsistencies, into which the state has been led in the effort to maintain its identity while adapting itself to conditions that challenge the validity of the attempt. The world passed through periods of drastic change before; the sixteenth century, to cite but one example, was one such passage that opened the gates to the kind of world we know. But historical parallels, like the supposed lessons of history, are fallacious guides. We are facing some wholly unprecedented circumstances, of which the state of weaponry is but the most dramatic aspect. As usual the shape of the future is wrapped in uncertainty; depending on one's disposition, one may look upon it with hope unlimited or with profound anguish. Perhaps we should settle for saying that it is distressingly fascinating.

NOTES

1. Tolstoy's *War and Peace* first appeared in 1865-69. Raymond Aron's *Paix et guerre entre les nations* was published in 1962 (4th. ed., 1966). An English translation, *Peace and War,* was issued in 1966; an abridged version in 1973.

2. The eighteenth-century partition of Poland is the classical exam-

ple. More recently, the three small Baltic states between Poland and Finland have been absorbed into the Soviet Union. This last instance is particularly relevant to the present discussion, the justification of it, officially at least, being on ideological grounds rather than on considerations of power.

3. One such empire alone persists, the Soviet Union, the continuation of the Russian empire of the tsars. On the rationale of this situation, see n. 2.

4. This, to be sure, applies to Western mankind only. The conditions of the time, the state of communications for one, made possible the simultaneous existence of two distinct centers, the Roman and the Chinese, with but minimal contacts between the two.

5. It is of course true that the change had already taken place in England, and the influence of English thought and example on French political thinkers was considerable. And it is also true that the American Revolution antedates the French. However, America was at the time too small and too far away, and as to England, the fact remains that it was the French Revolution that launched the democratic movement on its broader course; the phrase, "when Paris catches cold, Europe sneezes," aptly expressed this during the nineteenth century.

6. Guizot to de Broglie (the foreign minister), 23 September 1840. François Guizot, *Mémoires pour servir à l'histoire de mon temps* (Paris, 1858-67), vol. V, p. 371. Italics added.

7. This is a sweeping generalization, of which the English case itself, where socialism achieved but little response, may be seen as contrary evidence. Yet in the larger world picture the validity of the generalization may be accepted.

8. For a brief interval in 1919, when a Bolshevik regime was in control in Hungary, and in Germany too, it was feared that communism might succeed, a possibility for which the Russians held much hope and that they encouraged.

9. Hope for it was not necessarily abandoned, as witness the Russian assistance to the Chinese revolution in the twenties. But that experiment went wrong from the Russian point of view.

10. See above, n. 2, 3.

11. Initially at least, the newly emerged countries tended to copy the political institutions of their former masters. But that has not meant either continued adherence to democratic practices or alignment with American policy.

12. Except in the case of Finland, which retained its independence. In Poland, Russia recovered territory only as far as the Curzon Line, the

boundary suggested at one point in connection with the Polish-Soviet War of 1920-21. In the Far East, on the other hand, the losses of the Russo-Japanese War of 1904-05 have also been recovered.

13. In the July 1947 issue of the magazine *Foreign Affairs* there appeared an article, "The Sources of Soviet Conduct," written by George F. Kennan, although anonymously published at first, that may be said to have launched the idea of containment as a desirable American policy.

14. There is no need to enlarge upon the divisive effect of the Vietnam War on the American body politic. The support of such regimes as that which obtained in Greece until 1974, the involvement in the Chilean coup, and other instances that could be cited have operated to the same effect, giving rise to criticism at once legitimate and, from another standpoint, irrelevant.

15. Raymond Aron in *The Imperial Republic* (Englewood Cliffs, N.J., 1974) makes the important point that in the process of becoming an empire the United States has not espoused imperialism.

16. Considerable theoretical discussion is going on within the Communist fold. For obvious reasons it flourishes most freely among Communists in the free world and in a country like Yogoslavia. A good illustration of such thinking is the book by Roger Garaudy, *The Turning Point of Socialism* (London, 1970). Garaudy was a leading member of the politbureau of the French Communist party, from which position he was expelled for his pains.

5.

Communist Ideology and the Strategy of Detente
Harold C. Hinton

Lenin, the founding father of the theory and practice of Communist foreign policy and international relations, believed in the likelihood of an ultimate clash between the "camps" of "imperialism" and "socialism." But this was a view of the long-term future, and it is of greater practical importance that he perceived the existing strategic inferiority of his own side and the consequent necessity to seek "peaceful coexistence," in the sense of the avoidance of a dangerous level of armed conflict, with the adversary for at least as long as this unfavorable relationship persisted. To him peaceful coexistence, or detente, was wholly consistent in principle with the continuous or at least frequent application by the "socialist camp" of revolutionary politico-military pressures in ways not likely to evoke massive retaliation from "imperialism."

Abundant historical evidence, of which the Soviet-Cuban foray into Angola is a dramatic recent example, shows that Lenin's view has remained that of practically all leftists who consider themselves Marxist-Leninists, or Maoists, and not merely Marxists. There have been two major developments unforeseen by Lenin, however, that have modified without really transforming the traditional Leninist view of the relationship between the "socialist" and "imperialist" sides.

One is the advent of nuclear and thermonuclear weapons that has raised potentially to infinity the cost of a miscalculation of the threshold below which probing the "imperialist" position can occur without fatal results.

The other is the Sino-Soviet dispute. Lenin never visualized a challenge to the ideological and political authority of the Soviet party and state from another member of the "socialist camp" of sufficient proportions to constitute a rival claim to authority and to divide the Communist world into hostile factions, whether tightly or—as is increasingly the case—loosely organized ones. He could not foresee that this challenge would reach such a level as to cause the Soviet Union by 1969 to apply a level of military threats and pressures to the unruly Chinese sufficient to push them from being the more hostile to American "imperialism" to being the less hostile of the two great Communist powers, and indeed to seeking detente with the United States as a means, among other things, of counterbalancing the pressures from Soviet "social-imperialism." This Chinese approach to the United States, and the anticipation of it, were undoubtedly among the major causes of a similar and competitive Soviet approach to the United States of which some important early landmarks are the beginning of the SALT talks in November 1969 and the intensification of Soviet interest in economic and technical contacts following the Polish riots of December 1970.

The very fact that this situation is highly unorthodox by the standards of Marxist-Leninist ideology, as well as the obvious political and diplomatic advantages it tends to confer on the United States, creates at least a theoretical presumption that the two Communist rivals may decide to reconcile their differences to some significant degree. But the possibility appears in reality to be little more than theoretical. The Soviet side clearly wants a reconciliation, but on its own terms, and these probably include, and are perceived in Peking as including, a degree of subordination on the Chinese side—Soviet "advisers," for example—that is unacceptable. Peking lived for the decade of the 1950s as a rather, although decreasingly, close partner of the Soviet Union, with often unpleasant results and has no desire to repeat the experience, nor does Moscow appear to have the combination of strength and will necessary to coerce Peking into resuming such a relationship. Furthermore, the Chinese intensely resent the bullying to which they have been subjected by the Soviet Union since 1969. Just as the United States could not achieve anything better than an adversary relationship with the People's Republic of China as long as it was perceived in Peking, rightly or wrongly, as bullying and threatening it, as was the case down to the mid-1960s, so Moscow is unlikely to be able to achieve anything better than an adversary relationship unless and until it does something much more drastic than it has done so far to change its image in Peking as a threat and bully. These considerations are more compelling than purely ideological ones, and in any case ideology has been a divisive rather than a unifying factor in the Sino-Soviet relationship and is probably a declining force now that each side has either entered a period of generational leadership change (as in the Chinese case) or is about to enter one (as in the Soviet case).

Moscow would clearly have preferred a debilitating succession struggle in China after Mao Tse-tung's death and has been considerably distressed by the impressive success of the Yeh Chien-ying-Hua Kuo-feng leadership in consolidating its position and eliminating at least the most prominent of the Maoist radicals. In an effort to reach an accommodation with the new Chinese leadership, or at least to prevent it from locking itself into an anti-Soviet posture, Moscow has made a variety of overtures to Peking since Mao's death. So far as can be judged, these have failed, and Chinese domestic and foreign propaganda still denounces Soviet "social-imperialism" more bitterly than it attacks American "imperialism."

Meanwhile, Moscow and Peking continue to seek competitive detente with the United States, subject to the classical Leninist imperative to gain advantages for national and revolutionary interest at American expense where feasible and reasonably safe. The problem for the United States and other non-Communist countries, obviously, is to present the fewest possible vulnerabilities that may tempt the Communist powers from the path of detente into that of aggressiveness. The problem is easy to state but far from easy to solve. Clearly it is imperative that the Soviet Union not be permitted to gain a significant margin of strategic superiority over the United States. If it did, the original rationale of peaceful coexistence would tend to disappear, with results that are impossible to predict but would almost certainly be most unpleasant to experience.

6.

Ideology and Soviet Foreign Policy
Seweryn Bialer

The question of the relationship between ideology and Soviet foreign policy has never been resolved and probably never will be. The lack of resolution and clarity on this subject can be attributed not only to the lack of available and testable data but primarily to the fact that no clearcut answer is possible: The influence of ideology on human affairs in general and on foreign policy in particular is highly ambiguous. It seems, therefore, that any general answer to the question can be of importance only in providing a framework within which one can discuss the specific dimensions of the influence of ideology on Soviet foreign policy and discern secular trends that may have developed in that relationship during particular periods. In doing so, one should try to avoid the trap of analyzing the influence of ideology on foreign policy as predetermined in the past and preordained for the future, that is, as inherent in the nature of the Soviet system solely and not dependent on external realities, feedback, and actions.

I regard the remarks that follow as an introduction to discussion and will therefore be selective in what I shall cover. I shall address myself to three sets of issues. First, I shall explore what questions are involved in the subject of ideology and Soviet foreign policy. In some respects, this is the most difficult part of the inquiry because how one formulates the questions largely determines the answers that one gets. Second, I shall discuss why questions relating to the influence of ideology on Soviet foreign policy are being asked again with some urgency; why a subject that has been discussed so many times before is being explored anew, and what is new about it. And third, I shall suggest some answers to the questions concerning the influence of ideology on Soviet foreign policy, especially those elements of the relationship I consider distorted in the past or pertinent today.

To begin with, questions that can be and usually are raised regarding Soviet foreign policy are of two types. The first group of questions involves Soviet capabilities—that is, the resources that the Soviet Union has at its disposal in conducting its foreign policy and the projection of those capabilities into the future. One would like to know how Soviet capabilities are developed, how fast they are increasing, in what areas, and in what specific aspects. Ideology may have an influence on both the perception and the development of capabilities. But, I would argue, when we consider the relationship of ideology to foreign policy, we are not so much concerned with Soviet foreign policy resources and capabilities *per se* as with the purposes to which these capabilities may be applied. As John Strachey has remarked:

> It is a military maxim that in framing a country's defense policy the capabilities alone never the intentions of other nations must be taken into account. But this is one of those maxims, which however dutifully they are preached in the staff colleges, can never be adhered to in the cabinet rooms.[1]

Evidently, the United States and the Western alliance as a whole think and worry about Soviet capabilities today because they are worried about Soviet intentions. If we did not worry about intentions, we obviously would not be as concerned as we are about the pronounced expansion of Soviet foreign policy resources. It seems clear to me, therefore, that when we raise questions about the relationship between ideology and Soviet foreign policy, we are really predominantly interested in the second set of questions, questions involving Soviet intentions rather than their capabilities and foreign policy resources.

Three questions concerning Soviet foreign policy intentions are of particular importance. First is the straightforward question of how the Soviet Union intends to use its existing and developing foreign policy capabilities. When one asks this question, it is not at all necessary to posit some kind of a "master plan" or long-range strategy that ideology imposes on Soviet foreign policy, for it is doubtful that any such "plan" or "strategy" exists now or ever existed in the past. But what one can and should inquire about is whether there exists a long or intermediate-term predisposition among Soviet policymakers—whether there are some preferences and predilections in Soviet foreign policy planning—that can be referred to as a long-range intentions. And here the analysis of the ideological orientation of the policymakers can tell us a great deal. Such an analysis cannot tell us whether the Soviets will use the foreign policy capabilities that they have in any particular way. But it can provide clues as to how they are *inclined* to use those capabilities.

The second question involving intentions is: Why? That is, once one comes to a conclusion about long-range Soviet predilections and predispositions in foreign policy, then the question arises: What are the sources of those intentions? And here again the ideological orientation of Soviet policymakers is relevant not only analytically but for our own policy as well. Analytically, the issue is whether the Soviet predisposition toward a specific type of behavior is connected with the characteristics of a particular generation of leaders or, let us say, with the politics of an oligarchy, or whether the predisposition is primarily structural, rooted in a system of institutions and beliefs. In other words, the analytical problem involves determining how deeply a particular pattern of Soviet behavior is ingrained in the structure of a political society or in the political leadership. Clearly, our evaluation of this problem will have important policy implications because it will provide clues as to how to react to particular Soviet actions.

These considerations bring us to the third and broadest question concerning the impact of ideology on Soviet foreign policy intentions. This question involves the nature of the Soviet nation state. The Soviet nation state, as we well know, was created to fulfill a mission. It was founded to be a refuge, a bastion, a base of revolution for the whole world. Historical experience suggests that nation states with missions are apt to be even more self-assertive and aggressive than are nation states that do not place high values on any particular ideological and international ties, duties, or responsibilities. And it seems unquestionable that what the Soviet Union has in fact been during most of its existence is a nation state with a mission. I would argue that in the past, even when its leaders have most ruthlessly sacrificed the direct interests of Communist parties in the rest of the world—and they did sacrifice those interests, without any doubt—they have done so often in the belief that by preserving and strenghtening the Soviet Union at all costs, they were in the long run furthering the interests of communism all over the world. The question now, however, is to what extent the Soviet Union of the 1970s is, or the Soviet Union of the 1980s will be, a nation state of such special character.

In sum, the central issues in the relationship between ideology and Soviet foreign policy involve the nature of Soviet foreign policy intentions, the sources of those intentions, and the nature of the Soviet state. From this perspective, it is not at all difficult to understand the renewed interest in this relationship. The reasons for this reawakened interest and for the sense of urgency that underlines it are numerous and interconnected. Some of the reasons are old, some are new, but in their combination and intensity, they are clearly unique to the contemporary period. Some of the most important ones are listed below.

— The first and most obvious is the level of Soviet international capabilities already achieved. It is one thing to discuss the influence of ideology, however expansionist and self-assertive, on the foreign policy of a weak or at least of a clearly inferior Soviet state and quite another to consider the intentions of a Soviet Union that has attained strategic parity with the United States and has achieved the position of a global power. Under such circumstances when one is inquiring into the influence of ideology on Soviet foreign policy, one is asking in fact whether the achievement by the Soviet Union of global great power status parallels the development of more responsible and responsive Soviet behavior in the international arena, or whether that achievement can be described as a Soviet dream come true, an opportunity at last to push long-held and long-unfulfilled ambitions. The influence of ideology alone on Soviet foreign policy clearly can suggest only a part of the answer. But just as clearly it is highly relevant to the whole answer.

— A closely related reason and the key explanation for the sense of urgency that has lately become almost an obsession with Western policymakers is the question: Why is the Soviet Union arming at a pace that by any standard has to be considered extremely high? Overshadowing all of the disagreements about the level of Soviet capabilities already achieved and its projected military strength vis-à-vis the West is the question "Why?" In attempting to answer this question the evaluation of Soviet intentions looms as absolutely crucial. The unprecedented Soviet armament effort may be partly a response to past nightmares, to traumas of past insecurities that push the Soviets relentlessly toward the unattainable and often counterproductive goal of total and complete security, or what one can call "oversecurity." It may be an attempt to overcompensate, in the only area of real Soviet competence and achievements, for political and economic weaknesses at home and abroad. But it can also be explained as an attempt to achieve global military superiority, reflecting the belief of the Soviet leadership that such superiority is not only attainable but can also be translated into political power and influence. And, again, consideration of the question of ideology may help to explain both Soviet goals in the arms race and Soviet perceptions of its possible and desirable payoffs.

— Another reason for the urgent interest in Soviet foreign policy intentions and their ideological underpinnings involves recent Soviet actions, particularly their Angolan adventure. Their use of surrogate Cuban troops in a local civil war so far from their own shores is for the Soviet Union an unprecedented action—the first example of this kind of Soviet behavior in the international arena. Soviet policy in Angola could turn out to be no more than an episode, a very limited action taken because of the very low risk involved in an intervention at that particular time (for example, the state of American foreign policy and of the American polity in general and the South African intervention in Angola that made Soviet intervention acceptable to other African states), and because of the internal pressures of Soviet politics. Yet there is the probability that the Angolan action will remain not an exception but rather the beginning of a new pattern of behavior, reflecting growing Soviet capabilities and deeply seated predilections that will push Soviet action in this interventionist direction.

— The search for explanations of Soviet international behavior and foreign policy intentions is also related to the discernible change in the Soviet attitude toward detente. This is not to say that there is evidence that the Soviet leadership does not want detente to continue, but, first, that their initial expectations of the benefits of *cooperation* with the Western powers and especially with the United States have clearly been lowered and remain largely unfulfilled especially in the economic sphere, and second, that a change has occurred in Soviet expectations about detente from defensive to offensive, that is, the Soviets now stress the benefits that can be derived from cooperation less than the benefits that can accrue from competition with the West. As a result, the general level of cooperation within the framework of detente is being lowered vis-à-vis early Soviet intentions and Western expectations. Such a change may be connected with the Soviet perception of the crisis in industrial democracies (which the Soviet leadership did not envisage when detente was being shaped), with the resulting revitalization of their own ideological expectations about the decline of the West and the temptation that this produces for an activist, interventionist Soviet foreign policy.

The whole set of circumstances in which the question of Soviet foreign policy intentions and their ideological underpinnings again looms so large is related not only to Western perceptions of the present but even more to those of the future. A forceful argument can be made that current international trends point to an almost inescapable increase in global tension, turmoil, conflict, and uncertainty. If this proves to be the case, then global cooperation and the gradual institutionalization of cooperation between big powers will become more urgent than ever before. And here again the question of the impact of ideology on Soviet foreign policy is asked with some urgency because that impact is relevant to how the Soviet leadership will react to those global tensions and turmoil. Will they—aware of the dangers to them as well as to us—respond constructively to defuse tensions and dampen conflict and thus effectively commit themselves to the maintenance of order in the international system (even if it is an order that they cannot dominate)? Or will they see international instability as a dream come true, as a vindication of long-held hopes and a balm for long-felt frustrations? That is, will the Soviets perceive global disorder as a danger or as an opportunity—an opportunity to be used in attempting to replace the United States as the pivot of the international system?

Clearly, ideology alone will not answer these questions. One can again repeat that ideological influences on Soviet foreign policy are highly ambiguous, on the one hand, making the Soviets extraordinarily conscious of their own security and hence hesitant to take risks and, on the other hand, prompting them to see their global expansion in terms of a mission legitimized by "history itself," therefore reinforcing their desire to capitalize on their growing international capabilities and power.

But it is equally clear that the global situation is now—and will be increasingly in the future—qualitatively different from what we have known in the past. Not only will the Soviet Union be presented with unprecedented opportunities to exploit global anarchy and turmoil but its available and developing foreign policy resources, both absolutely and relative to the West, will give it unprecedented means to do so. Under such circumstances—marked by a vivid American sense of the limitations of the power of the United States, by the decline of West European influence in world affairs, and by the rapid growth of Soviet capabilities to intervene, directly or through surrogates, in areas far removed from its borders—we cannot rely entirely on past Soviet international behavior either to divine Soviet intentions in the present or to predict them for the future. The circumstances that now prevail underscore the importance of taking a new look at the relationship between ideology and Soviet foreign policy.

There is another major reason why the question of the

relationship of ideology and Soviet foreign policy is so important today. This has to do with the incongruity between our image of the Soviet internal system, on the one hand, and our anxieties about present and future Soviet international behavior, on the other. When we speak about the Soviet Union internally, the picture that we have, and I think correctly, is of a system in which Communist doctrine has lost its operational importance. Communist doctrine remains one of the legitimizing principles of the Soviet internal system, particularly for the elites, but it is hardly an operational principle that still exercises a major influence on Soviet internal policies. Domestically, the Soviet Union is one of the most status quo oriented countries in the world. Of all industrial countries, it is undoubtedly the most frozen, conservative, and Victorian in its political, socioeconomic, and cultural relations. Its oppressiveness is no longer oriented toward reshaping society but toward preserving the mold into which the society was shaped. And yet when one discusses Soviet foreign policy intentions and asks about the impact of ideology on Soviet international behavior, one tends to think in terms of a revolutionary ideology, most particularly Communist doctrine. Thus the incongruity that emerges between the two images of the Soviet Union—the internal and the external—seems to be pronounced.

One other phenomenon invests the paradox posed above with an additional dimension that makes it even more complex and pronounced. The Soviet system as an emulative revolutionary model belongs basically to the past; in the present, it is dead for all practical purposes. Even those major Communist or radical parties that still declare some allegiance to the Soviet Union do not consider the Soviet model applicable to their own societies. But, most crucially, the process of radicalization, the growth of militancy in the world, is not at all proceeding in a pro-Soviet direction; it does not have a pro-Soviet effect. In a growing number of cases, as specific strata, movements, and even nation states become more and more militant, they tend to evolve as much in an anti-Soviet as in an anti-American, anti-West, and anticapitalist direction. And, therefore, the dilemma of how a nation and a system can at the same time be reactionary internally and have revolutionary goals externally is supplemented by another dilemma: Can it be sufficiently revolutionary externally to satisfy the new world militancy without endangering its own stability and its internal reactionism? Of course, we can still hypothesize that the Soviet Union remains a nation state with a mission, but the question then becomes: What is the mission? The paradox described is real: It reflects one of the built-in dilemmas of Soviet international behavior and intentions.

I shall now suggest some partial answers to some of the questions that I have raised. First, the question of the influence of ideology on the perceptions and outlook of the Soviet leadership and political elite raises the entire complex of problems expressed by the concept of the "erosion" and even the "end of ideology." The "end" of Soviet ideology has occurred so many times in the past fifty years that its burial should have long since been forgotten. If one is waiting for the end of ideology and not for its change, then the warning of Clifford Geertz that one may wait for it as long as the positivists waited for the end of religion is much to the point.[2] The "end of ideology" theme is misleading insofar as it implies that the political realism dominant in the thinking of the contemporary Soviet elite is devoid of ideology because not only is it not associated with serious theorizing but it is even adverse to it.

It is as nonsensical to view the contemporary Soviet political elite as revolutionary fanatics whose every major policy or act is colored by the ultimate ends as prescribed by Marxist and Leninist holy writ as it is to see them only as cynical manipulators who simply drift toward undefined goals and whose response to reality is not influenced by their intellectual and political revolutionary origins. The question is not whether their beliefs have changed but which beliefs, how much, and in what direction; not whether they have an ideology but to what ideology they subscribe; not whether ideology makes any difference but what kind of difference it makes for the shaping of their intentions, policies, and behavior.

This is not the place to get bogged down in a discussion of the meaning of "ideology." I prefer to understand "ideology" in its broader meaning, and it seems to me that most students of belief systems would probably agree that the concept should include much more than purely doctrinal elements. One may distinguish various dimensions and levels of ideology. The most basic of these is doctrinal, what Franz Schurmann terms "the pure ideology." Whatever distortions of selectivity, interpretation, or addition occurred during the Soviet's development of Marxian theory and of Bolshevism, Marxism-Leninism is still the core of this pure ideology. On this ideological level, the basic tendency of the last ten to fifteen years has been that of ideological retrenchment and increasing ritualization.

The retrenchment finds its expression in the disappearance of ideological innovations, in the treatment of the central questions of Soviet history, in the very dogmatic, uncritical, monotonous tenor of the textbooks, pamphlets, and so forth used in mass and party indoctrination, and, most importantly, in the lack of any serious effort to go beyond routine in the attempt to propagate the doctrine to nonbelievers or doubters. Instead, the emphasis has been on resistance to and defense against "alien ideas." The increasing ritualization finds its most important expression in the fact that the doctrinal position on policy issues is ambiguous, nonauthoritative, and ill defined. Policy discussions, therefore, are conducted neither against a doctrinal prescription nor in support of it but parallel to doctrine. Direct doctrinal intervention in expert deliberations is limited, and thereby the desire to issue binding verdicts on policy questions that are unresolved or unclear is curtailed. Thus, the doctrine can retain a semblance of consistency, and disagreements about its meaning and consequences for action are minimized by keeping it increasingly aloof from social practice—that is, by the increased ritualization of doctrine.

With respect to foreign policy questions and to the analysis of international relations, attacks from both the left and the right in the Communist movement and from the radical community have brought about a revitalization of Soviet doctrinal writings. Angry and concerned about these attacks, the Soviet leaders have responded by reaffirming their international "revolutionary" doctrine and their commitment to the "world revolutionary process." The form and substance of this reaffirmation is very aptly described by Alexander Dallin:

> What the thrust of reformulations and redefinitions amounts to in practice is a persistent widening of options; it brings the substitution of vaguer, weaker, broader terms and categories, the elimination of compelling cause-and-effect relationships, and a withering of the fundamental optimism about the future which animated the movement at the start. 'The world revolutionary process becomes ever more complex and multiform,' declares a recent Soviet study of the problem. In substance, the belief system now sanctions the view that anything is possible. Any one thing may or may not occur; revolutions may or may not take place; force may or may not be needed; communists may or may not be in control of 'bourgeois' or 'mass democratic' movements; non-Western countries may or may not opt for a noncapitalist path, which in turn may or may not lead to socialist revolution. . . . The multiplicity of labels, options, forms, alliances, and combinations continues to grow. Given such a broad range, which in advance foresees and justifies all success and all failure, Soviet doctrine (which thus cannot be falsified) becomes useless as an analytical or predictive tool. It is rather a distorted reflection of a politi-

cal system trying to come to terms with the present without betraying its past.[3]

In sum, the process of ritualization regarding doctrinal inputs in foreign policy is advanced. There is no evidence whatsoever that revolutionary prospects abroad constitute controlling factors in Soviet foreign policy decisions and in Soviet leadership intentions in the international arena.

Yet the question of the influence of ideology on policy should concern itself primarily not with "pure" but with "practical" ideology—the ideas, principles, and preferences that provide the dominant conceptual *framework* of elite intentions and actions, the matrix of its collective conscience. "Practical" ideology continues to be influenced by doctrine not only in its symbolic expressions (language, terminology, emotive meanings) but also in substance. Increasingly, however, its influence is mainly negative: Doctrine rules out certain options in decision making and reinforces or weakens the arguments against others. For instance, it reinforces Soviet resistance to change in Eastern Europe; ideologically based conceptions of the state have a great deal to do with Soviet insistence on regimes that are not merely friendly but Communist. But doctrinal influence is only one influence on "practical" ideology, the dominant source of which is the tradition of the Soviet system—the historical experience of the political elite itself. This is especially true of those elements of "practical ideology" that are directly relevant to the political process. I shall mention some of the most important elements that form the perceptions and basic political outlook of the "practical ideology" that constitutes the "collective conscience" of the Soviet leadership and political elite, stressing whenever possible the direction of its evolution in the post-Stalin and the post-Khrushchev era and indicating if at all pertinent the foreign policy manifestations of such an evolution.

First, the withering away of utopia and utopianism in the

thought and practice of the political elite has been accelerated. This Soviet utopianism, the strongest and closest deriva-
tive of the doctrinal tradition, continued to constitute under
Khrushchev one part of the vision of the future within which
the elite operated. The contemporary Soviet leadership, however, dislikes and discourages the futuristic "Communist"
fantasy. Realism and businesslike behavior have become
their ubiquitous slogans and the leadership qualities that are
most praised in the written and spoken word.

Second, the elite impulse to reshape society has radically
declined. For the ruling elite, Soviet social structure has
found its permanent shape—at least for the foreseeable future. What the party proposes to the Soviet population is
nothing but the indefinite continuation of the basic existing
social relations plus material progress. The innovative impulse
of the political elite is focused entirely on functioning innovations not on restructuring innovations.

Third, generations of Soviet leaders have assimilated from
the Marxian tradition the dimension that it shared with Western rationalism: the belief in progress. The decline in the
West of the attractiveness of the idea of progress has not been
duplicated in the Soviet Union. True, the optimism of the
Khrushchev era has been replaced by a more somber assessment and by a much greater realism about what can be
achieved in the short and intermediate terms. The future
looks less like unilinear, unbridled progress. But what has
changed very little is the deeply entrenched belief in and
commitment to continuous economic growth and to the all-
pervading technological ethos.

Fourth, the persistent centrality of the belief in progress
and its almost total equation with material growth are associated with and supplemented by a deeply-rooted attitude of
evaluating one's performance in "progressing to progress" by
the standards of Western industrial nations. The sources of
this "comparative" mentality are many: Justification of the

past history of sacrifice and denial, ultimate legitimation of the superiority of the system, and the felt need to ensure the security of the system from alien and hostile external forces. Regardless of the specific sources of this mentality, however, the important point to note is that it has taken hold in all segments of the Soviet elite and thus has acquired an existence of its own. This mentality infuses into the political elite a sense of urgency and a stress on mobilization that persist not only when a growing lag in comparison with the performance of Western industrial societies is discernible but even in times of notable achievement.

Fifth, the thinking and behavior of the Soviet leadership and political elite are still dominated by a set of beliefs and attitudes that expresses deep-seated fear and mistrust of spontaneity in political and social behavior, inducing an interventionist psychology and placing a premium on strong central government, organization, and order.

Last (and crucial from the point of view of foreign policy), the mainstay of the Soviet political elite's sense of common purpose is provided more than ever by nationalism. Partly in its great power Soviet dimension, and partly in its cultural, traditional Russian dimension, this nationalism constitutes the major effective, long-lasting bond within the political elite and between the elite and the masses. The old conservative theme—the cult of national unity and the condemnation of individuals and groups who threaten to impair it—provides the emotional base for an authoritarian political outlook and is in turn reinforced by it.

The elements of the dominant "practical ideology" described above have numerous implications for Soviet thinking, intentions, and behavior in international relations. The decisive decline in Soviet utopianism is reflected in foreign policy behavior that manifests pragmatism, gradualism, and deliberateness, puts a premium on a strict realistic evaluation of the attractiveness of specific goals in terms of available resources, and shuns shortcuts and grandstanding. Despite the fact that the paranoic isolationism and insecurities of the Stalinist era belong largely to the past, the reactionary Soviet attitude toward changes in the internal sociopolitical structure makes for a pronounced and apparently growing sensitivity and sense of vulnerability to possible deleterious and destabilizing external influences on the Soviet domestic scene. This seems especially the case now, when contacts with the outside world are being extended, when many of the barriers to international communication are being lowered, and when internal pressures for changes and improvements at home are rising. The centrality of the goal of material and technological progress as the raison d'être of the Soviet system is paralleled, as mentioned above, by the continuing tendency to assess Soviet achievements by the measuring rod of Western material and technological standards (accompanied by a disdain and contempt for Western spiritual achievements and sociopolitical organization). The effects of such a combination are twofold: On the one hand, in view of a lack of commitment to internal reforms that may improve techno-economic performance, it pushes the Soviet leadership to seek highly expanded and improved economic relations with the industrialized West; on the other hand, it leads the Soviet political elite to push in the one area of development in which they have real strength and, *nolens volens,* to rely inordinately on those foreign policy resources that are available and solid—that is, military resources. Military development is no longer the sole goal of Soviet economic expansion as it was in Stalin's time. Despite Khrushchev's hopes of catching up with the West on a broad economic front, however, the military sector remains the only internationally competitive sector, the only visible and measurable achievement of the Soviet system, and the key competitive international resource at the Soviet leadership's disposal.

Although all of the above factors are important in themselves, the absolutely crucial relation of "practical ideology" to Soviet foreign policy intentions and behavior has to do with the question of the nature and influence of Soviet nationalism. But when stressing the importance of nationalism as the central component of the "practical ideology" that informs the attitudes, intentions, and actions of the Soviet political elite, it is not sufficient to speak about it in a general way. What is required is the identification of its specifically Soviet character.

There are three major components that in their mutual interaction constitute the determining characteristics of Soviet nationalism today. First, it is partly a nationalism shaped by the past experiences of the Soviet Union and Russia that can best be characterized as defensive in nature. It is a nationalism that grew out of the traumatic experiences of being so often invaded, of being weak, of being beaten or even nearly destroyed. It is a nationalism that stresses the separateness of Russia from other nations and the unbridgeability of the "we-they" syndrome in international relations and that shapes the total and unusually intense preoccupation with national security, with safe borders, with preparedness to repulse a world that is axiomatically assumed to be at least potentially hostile.

It is also partly and in an undiminished degree still an imperial nationalism—in all probability the last one left on the globe. It is a nationalism committed to an empire that Stalin built in Eastern Europe, the existence and integrity of which his successors have continued to defend at all costs. In this dimension it is a nationalism that expands the basically defensive preoccupation with security to include not only the Soviet Union proper but the whole Eastern European area of uncontested Soviet influence. It is as if the slogan "socialism in one country," under which Stalinism was established in the Soviet Union, was expanded by Stalin himself after the Second World War into "socialism in one empire" and is accepted with no sign of diminished commitment by his successors.

Last, and most important for the future of international relations, it is to an increasing degree the nationalism of a great power that has attained global stature. It is the nationalism of a power that is still young, growing, ambitious, and assertive and that still entertains hopes for and illusions about what the application of great power in the international arena can accomplish. It is a nationalism of the older generation of Soviet leaders who worked so hard, waited so long, and hoped so intensely for the Soviet Union to achieve a dominant international position, those who only now have begun to see the complications and limitations of their newly acquired status, and who still do not want to face up to the difficulties of translating their real power into tangible international awards and accomplishments. It is the nationalism of the younger postwar generation of Soviet leaders who share the ambitions of their elders but not the lingering insecurities and memories of past weaknesses, those who lack the maturing influence of knowing what past sacrifices meant and at what cost Soviet power was created.

In my opinion, the interaction of the dimensions of Soviet nationalism—Russian in substance and Soviet in form— constitutes the single most important explanatory factor in Soviet international behavior. However, what about the explanatory value of other constituent elements of Soviet "practical ideology" in analyzing the intentions and actions of Soviet foreign policy? How important in particular is the doctrinal component in such an analysis? This problem—the question of the relative importance of separate determinants of Soviet foreign policy, of their relative causal influence on the shape and direction of Soviet international behavior—is of course the most difficult one. No clearcut answer is possible; some general remarks will have to suffice.

The crucial point to be made here is that the distinctions

among the various elements of Soviet "practical ideology" depicted above—the doctrinal inputs, nationalism in its many dimensions, the authoritarian impulse, the reactionary attitude toward the Soviet sociopolitical organization and so forth—are in essence analytical distinctions that in real life are not necessarily separate, distinct, or counterposed to one another. Under certain conditions, these analytically separate elements, for example, doctrine and nationalism, are in reality inseparable. One can put them in separate chapters in a textbook on the sources of Soviet international behavior, but in reality they are meshed. They are meshed in the minds of the people who make policy, they are intertwined in the perceptions and feelings of the Soviet elites, and they cannot be separated when analyzing the elite's intentions and actions. Of course, particular groups and individuals within the Soviet political elite will differ in their devotion to particular doctrinal principles or pronouncements or in the intensity of their nationalistic feelings and commitments. I do not believe, however, that these differences are so clearcut as they are sometimes made out to be. It is a vast oversimplification, to take an extreme example, to counterpose a doctrinaire group of ideologues whose devotion to doctrinal ideology is supreme to, let us say, a military group composed of pure and simple nationalists. The differences among groups and individuals who make Soviet foreign policy are seldom of an either-or nature; rather, they are distinctions of degree.

The fundamental difficulty, then, is that the relative weight of the various elements and components of Soviet "practical ideology" can only be evaluated when these elements create tensions in the actual conduct of Soviet policy and policymaking—that is, when they conflict with one another. Often, however, the various components of Soviet "practical ideology" supplement and reinforce each other. In such cases, the distinctions that can be drawn among them are primarily analytical; factors are separated that in reality are meshed.

One such case is the Sino-Soviet conflict. In evaluating the sources that have influenced this conflict, how can we separate the doctrinal divisions from divergencies of national interest? The elements reinforce each other. Doctrinal differences and commitments, the belief of each side that it represents the truth, reinforce nationalism and the dislike and fear of one another. Indeed, it is this reinforcement that makes the conflict so intractable and its solution so particularly difficult.

Another example concerns the Soviet quest for absolute security. Here again nationalism and ideology in the narrow, doctrinal sense reinforce each other. As indicated before, the *defensive* dimension of Soviet nationalism provides a basis for the extraordinary Soviet preoccupation with security. But so does the ideology, with its view of the world as divided into hostile, irreconcilable camps and its view of the Soviet state as the "bastion of progress," the base of a system to which the future belongs. As Thomas Wolfe suggests, the main impact of the Marxist-Leninist doctrine on Soviet foreign policymakers is expressed in two tendencies: to see the world in terms of systemic struggle that cannot be "annulled" by intergovernmental agreements and to see that the security of the Soviet Union, as the principal Communist state, must be preserved at all costs. Writes Wolfe:

> The common denominator in both instances seems to lie in seeking to eliminate or reduce potential sources of threat to the Soviet Union. What might be called, in strategic parlance, a 'damage limiting' philosophy, thus seems to permeate Soviet behavior. . . . This philosophy finds expression in Soviet military doctrine and policy, as well as in Soviet diplomacy. Whether at bottom such a philosophy owes more to ideological imperatives than to those of Soviet national interest remains a moot question. For that matter, the impulse to limit damage to one's interests is not peculiar to the Soviet leaders; they simply seem to carry it far-

ther than most, as if satisfied only with absolute security.
Thus, the really relevant point seems to be that to the
extent that negation of potential military and political
threats to the Soviet Union involves measures that other
states find inimical to their own vital interests, the Soviet
proclivity to seek absolute security tends neither to promote global stability nor a fundamental relaxation of
tensions within the international order.[4]

Still another example is provided by the Soviet commitment to its East European empire. Soviet imperial nationalism by itself does not, in my opinion, explain the strength of
this commitment and its successful defense. Rather, one of
the very important long-range functions of doctrinal orthodoxy is tied to the Soviet imperial position in Eastern Europe
and to the Brezhnev doctrine of limited sovereignty that safe-
guards it ideologically. Doctrinal orthodoxy provides the sole
possible legitimization of the empire in the eyes of the Soviet
political elite, among some segments of the East European
party elites, and in some Communist parties outside the Soviet bloc. Of course, Soviet dominance of Eastern Europe
rests primarily on Soviet military power. But for the Soviet
elite to contemplate the use of that power, let alone actually
to use it, requires the evocation of the doctrinal right that
makes it "just."

Supplementation and reinforcement are, however, not the
only existing or possible relations among the component elements of Soviet "practical ideology." And when the various
elements do not supplement and reinforce each other, their
analytical separation can become a reality, when the various
inputs into the belief system may conflict and create tensions
and major crosspressures on Soviet foreign policymakers.
These major crosspressures, conflicts, and tensions sometimes
lead to greater militancy in Soviet foreign policy and sometimes to greater restraint. But they always create an ambiguity that does not exist when the component elements of

the Soviet "practical ideology" supplement and reinforce each other.

The conflicts, tensions, and ambiguities to which Soviet policymakers are exposed are at bottom tensions between what the Soviet leadership and political elite want, on the one hand, and what they fear, on the other; between the rewards that they hope for or expect and the risks that they must take to get them; between what Alex Dallin so aptly phrased as the impulse to enjoy and the impulse to destroy. Again, many examples can be provided for such tensions, conflicts, and ambiguities.

One of the areas in which the tensions and crosspressures on Soviet foreign policymakers are especially clear now concerns a major issue in European foreign policy, the question of Eurocommunism. The tensions and ambiguities intertwine on many levels. On one level, there is a tension between the opportunity implied in Eurocommunism to destabilize Western Europe and the Western alliance and to strengthen Communist influence in the major industrial countries of the West, on the one hand; and the fear of what successful Eurocommunism may do to detente, on the other. One aspect of this fear is that detente may be so undermined that the key Soviet economic interests motivating the pursuit of that policy as well as the quest for the control of nuclear armaments will be severely damaged. An even greater fear is the possibility of a miscalculation on the part of the European left that—instead of leading to the establishment of left or left-centered regimes in Western Europe—could lead instead to a powerful and successful reaction by the right and the recurrence, at least in part, of past Soviet nightmares about national security. On another level, it is the tension between the potential rewards to be reaped from, let us say, the success of the Italian Communist party and the potentially dangerous repercussions that a successful Italian party, authentically and continuously committed to democratic procedures, may create in Eastern Europe—an area, after all, much more important to the Soviet Union than is Italy.

In such situations—those in which Soviet policymakers are subject to severe tensions, conflicts, ambiguities, and cross-pressures—the relationship between ideology and Soviet foreign policy is both problematical and crucial. When there are tensions between rewards and risks or conflicts between different components of the "practical ideology," then the ways in which the Soviet leadership and political elite assign priorities to particular goals, rewards, or expectations take on special importance.

One may infer the order of priorities that becomes discernible in the long run from the conduct of Soviet foreign policy. I would divide these priorities basically into two groups. First, there are "absolute" priorities—the priorities that are almost constant attributes of Soviet international behavior at the highest order of importance. They have not changed perceptibly in the past and can be considered the minimal, irreducible requirements of Soviet foreign policy making. One such priority concerns the security of the Soviet home base—the security of the homeland and of Soviet rule within the homeland. The second such "absolute" priority concerns the security of the Soviet empire. I would suggest that in the perception of the Soviet leadership, the question of Communist rule and Soviet dominance in Eastern Europe is now considered basically an internal Soviet problem. The Soviet commitment is total, approaching in intensity its commitment to the defense and security of its own homeland. Until now, to a degree greater than is the case with any other major power, no step in Soviet foreign policy making was envisaged that could be thought to endanger the security of the Soviet homeland, the basic stability of the Soviet political elites' rule, or the stability of Soviet dominance in Eastern Europe. (This of course does not mean that some Soviet foreign policy actions did not in fact bring about such dangers as their unintended consequences; it means only that in the calculus of Soviet foreign policy making, leadership sensitivity to such dangers is extraordinarily developed.)

The second group of priorities I would describe as "relative"—the priorities that carry variable weight in Soviet foreign policy making and whose importance as determinants of Soviet international behavior changes sometimes very quickly and perceptively. Here I would include, in the first place, the goal of enhancing Soviet political influence in the international arena. This goal is reflected particularly in attempts to establish through bilaterial relations strong ties of dependence with individual strategically located countries and to foster, support, and encourage governments friendly to the Soviet Union and to its international positions. Efforts to attain such goals may focus in different periods on diverse areas of the world. But in this regard the most important characteristic of Soviet policy in the last decade, reflecting its developing global power status, is that it is not limited to any specific area. These efforts are partly defensive in nature, directed at achieving the retreat and isolation of recognized hostile powers or unfriendly competitors for influence (for example, China and the United States) and partly offensive, directed at gaining a strong foothold in building up a solid base of support in particular areas of the world. The major policy forms through which these goals are pursued are primarily political (for example, a quid pro quo of Soviet support for the solution of a specific grievance of a country for that country's support of Soviet positions in a particular area of the world), particularly economic (for example, economic aid), and indirectly to a very large extent, military (for example, supply of weapons including weapons systems and licensing and military instruction teams).

Another such relative priority would include the economic goals of developing the inflow of technology from industrialized capitalist countries, of securing sources of agricultural imports, and of obtaining credits from and cooperative economic arrangements with the West. In the last decade this Soviet goal has acquired a great deal of importance, becoming the necessary prerequisite of maintaining the desirable rate of growth of economic and particularly of industrial productivity without resorting to major internal economic reforms.

The priority, if the term is applicable at all, of revolutions abroad, of fostering and helping Communist takeovers, ranks probably rather low on the list. And here, of course, the degree of control that the Soviets hope or expect to have over the regimes which would emerge from such takeovers and the strategic importance of the countries themselves make an important difference in the extent of Soviet interest generated and in the type and scope of Soviet resources to be devoted to the enterprise. The above has to be distinguished from the goal of helping to sustain foreign Communist movements, on the one hand, and from trying to keep actual or at least symbolic control of these movements, on the other, a goal that still retains an important place among the "relative" priorities of Soviet international behavior.

The order of importance of the priorities described above is quite changeable; it is not set once and for all. The different weights attached to the various "relative" priorities depend on a number of factors. The key factors are the connections associated with and the influence exerted on absolute priorities. If, for example, a situation were to evolve in the Soviet Union in which the spread of consumerist attitudes among the working class reached a level where it seriously impaired economic performance, then the leadership—afraid of unrest that might endanger the internal stability of the regime—would probably elevate economic progress to the top of the list of "relative" priorities so that it acquired an importance close to that of "absolute" priorities.

It is clear, then, that ideology has provided neither a blueprint for Soviet decisionmakers nor a guide for Western scholars. It has served to create Soviet perceptions, inclinations, and predispositions that are frequently inconsistent among themselves and that rarely have unambiguous implications for action. Its impact has varied with time, place, and issue and cannot be assessed independently of numerous other factors that shape the character and direction of Soviet international behavior. However strong the influence of ideology in general and doctrine in particular has been on Soviet foreign policy in the past, both the policy and the ideology have always been conditioned by external realities, feedback, and actions.

Throughout its history, the Soviet Union has adapted its international behavior to the changing circumstances of world politics and to its own domestic conditions and requirements. Internationally, the Soviet Union's impressive military status barely obscures a very imbalanced great power status. Its military power is great, but its economic influence is minimal. Its political system attracts no admiration. Its revolutionary ideological attraction has waned. It exercises none of the cultural attractiveness of history's empires. The Soviet Union may be able to drive American influence out of various regions, but it cannot replace America as the pivot of international relationships.

Domestically, the hitherto dynamic Soviet economy's rate of growth is declining, and the technological gap between the Soviet Union and the West is becoming more and more evident. Despite extremely high rates of investment in agriculture, agricultural productivity continues to lag. Demographic trends complicate all of these problems: A looming labor shortage will strain the Soviet ability to maintain a huge labor-intensive agricultural sector, a very large army, a large educational sector needed to promote technological development, and a relatively labor-intensive industrial sector. Finally, although the Soviet Union so far has largely escaped the cultural/economic problems of both the West and the third world, that escape may be temporary because industrial development and exposure to mass consumption societies are creating a more self-conscious and assertive working class and may be stimulating a revolution of rising consumer expectations.

The Soviet Union remains a compound of enormous muscles and enormous insecurity. Both the muscles and the insecurity will continually increase. Unlike the malaise of the West, the Soviet malaise implies no decrease in foreign policy assertiveness or military budgets. As the malaise of the West has shaped much of the international relations of the past decade, the Soviet struggle to contain its emerging economic, cultural, political, and international malaise will shape much of the coming decade.

NOTES

1. John Strachey, "Communist Intentions" in *Partisan Review* XXIX, no. 2 (Spring 1962):215.

2. Clifford Geertz, "Ideology as a Cultural System" in *Ideology and Discontent,* ed. David E. Apter (New York, 1964), p. 51.

3. Alexander Dallin, "Retreat from Optimism: On Marxian Models of Revolution" in *Radicalism in the Contemporary Age,* vol. 3, *Strategies and Impact of Contemporary Radicalism,* eds. Seweryn Bialer and Sophia Sluzar (Boulder, Colorado, 1977).

4. Thomas W. Wolfe, "Military Power and Soviet Policy" in *The Soviet Empire: Expansion and Detente,* ed. William E. Griffith (Lexington, Mass., 1976), p. 149.

7.

Ideology and Chinese Foreign Policy
Donald S. Zagoria

In social scientific literature the concept of "ideology" is a swamp into which many analysts have journeyed but few have returned. There are at least two questions that evade even a minimum consensus. First is the question of how to define "ideology." Some students of the subject equate ideology with any value or belief system and thus define the concept so broadly as to render it virtually useless as an explanatory variable. Others, particularly students of Marxism and fascism, reserve the term for a structured, revolutionary doctrine that is associated with an organization such as a Communist or Fascist party. But to confine the concept of "ideology" to the revolutionary doctrine of Communist or Fascist parties begs most of the important questions. Do not non-revolutionary politicians and parties have "ideologies" that help to motivate their behavior? Is not liberalism an ideology? Do not "pragmatists" also have views about the world in which they live?

An even more fundamental question over which opinion is sharply divided concerns the relationship between ideas and behavior. There are two extreme views on this question. First is the view that human ideas are mere rationalizations of action motivated by other allegedly more "fundamental"

103

considerations, such as the pursuit of power or interests. Both Marxism and Freudianism have contributed to this tendency. But to dismiss ideology in this manner is to assume that power and interests exist in some "pure" form and have no relationship to the conscious ideas of individuals. Yet surely the ideas in the heads of powerholders influence the way in which they approach, use, and evaluate power.

The second extreme answer to this question is that ideology provides a more or less precise "guide to action," a ready-made book of rules. But no system of ideas can provide a precise guide to action in changing historical circumstances. The continuous disputes within Communist movements over the proper policy to pursue, the constant tendency toward schism, and the continual reevaluation of strategy in the face of changing circumstances all indicate that even a structured ideology cannot serve as a precise guide to action. Some analysts have sought to overcome this problem by differentiating between the "pure" and the "practical" ideology of Communist parties, or between the core doctrine and the day-to-day tactics. But this distinction does not go very far in helping to specify the ideological roots of behavior. How do we know that the "practical" ideology or tactics are at all related to the "pure" or "core" ideology?

Apart from these conceptual difficulties, there is yet another problem involved in relating Communist ideology to Communist behavior. We do not have access to the decision making process in any Communist party. Any proper analysis of the role of ideology in Chinese Communist foreign policy would have to be based on case studies of the Chinese decision-making process. What were the principal motivating ideas in the Chinese decision to enter into an alliance with the Soviet Union in 1950 and to break with the Soviet Union in 1960? What were the ideas motivating the Chinese to attack India in 1959? What were the ideas motivating the Chinese to enter into a detente with the United States in 1972?

If we had case studies based on interviews with the key Chinese leaders involved in making those decisions, we might be able to come to grips with the problem. But the fact is that we do not have such case studies and are unlikely to get them. Thus, any analysis of the motivating factors in Chinese policy must remain speculative.

In the analysis that follows, I am going to speculate on the motivations behind several key departures in Chinese foreign policy during the past twenty-five years. But before undertaking this analysis, I want to indicate how I propose to deal with the problems I stated earlier, the problem of defining ideology and the problem of trying to specify the relationship between ideas and behavior.

As I indicated, ideology can be defined either in the broad sense as values or it can be defined in the narrow sense as Communist revolutionary doctrine. Because the difficulties of trying to relate ideology in the broad sense to Chinese foreign policy—or, for that matter, to the foreign policy of any country—are simply too great, I propose to confine the meaning of ideology in this essay to the narrow definition. By "Maoist ideology," I mean Maoist revolutionary doctrine.

I propose to deal with the second problem by performing an experiment. I will try to explain Chinese foreign policy largely in nondoctrinal terms. If I succeed, I can conclude that Maoist revolutionary doctrine cannot provide the *focus* for explaining Chinese foreign policy.

To anticipate my conclusion, I do believe that most of Chinese foreign policy over the past twenty-five years can be explained in traditional terms such as the quest for security, the desire to maintain a "balance of power," and the desire to fulfill certain national interests. To anticipate my critics, I am *not* arguing that Maoist doctrine is irrelevant to an understanding of Chinese behavior. But I believe that doctrine may best be viewed as a supplementary rather than an independent variable in motivating Chinese foreign policy. Sometimes that doctrine reinforces the tendency of Chinese leaders to act in certain ways that they may deem necessary to secure their interests; at other times, that doctrine may conflict with their assessments of China's interests. In the former case, there is no problem. In the latter case, "interests" take precedence over doctrine. Thus, my argument is simply that doctrine cannot provide the main focus for explaining Chinese foreign policy, not that it is irrelevant.

We can begin to address this problem by examining in some detail a few of the major foreign policy decisions made by the Chinese Communists and speculating on the motivations of those decisions. Perhaps the first major foreign policy decision made by the Chinese Communists after they came to power was the decision to enter into an alliance with the Soviet Union. There can be little doubt but that *part* of the Chinese motivation for entering into this alliance with Moscow was ideological. At the time, the Chinese Communist party did consider itself to be part of a worldwide, revolutionary movement led by the Kremlin; it did accept much of the world view then prevalent among Communists in all countries; and it did regard the United States as the leading "imperialist" power.

On the other hand, China's desire for a military alliance with the Soviet Union in 1950 can also be explained on grounds of national security. By late 1948 and early 1949, the United States had begun to reevaluate the world situation in terms of the cold war with Russia and was coming to view the entire Communist world as an intransigent and monolithic enemy dedicated to the destruction of the free world. From 1947 to 1948, the United States actively intervened on the side of the Chinese Nationalists against the Communists in the Chinese civil war. And in the spring and fall of 1949, President Truman, fearful of the pro-Nationalist "China lobby" in the Congress, rejected overtures from the Chinese Communists for a dialogue and encouraged Western countries not to be hasty in recognizing the new Chinese government.[1] All of these actions must have reinforced the Chinese Communist image of the United States as a threat.

Moreover, by the end of 1948, the American reevaluation of the world situation was leading to a substantial change in United States policy toward Japan. The rate of occupation reform slowed down, some reforms were modified or abandoned, and Japan was increasingly being regarded by the United States as an ally in the new cold war rather than as a defeated enemy.

In sum, by the time that Mao delivered his "lean to one side" speech in July 1949, the United States had given the Chinese Communists ample indication that Washington regarded Peking as an implacable adversary aligned to the Soviet Union.

The crucial question then is: What would Chinese policy toward the United States and the Soviet Union have been if American policy toward the Chinese Communists had been more flexible? Several factors have to be taken into account. First, both Mao and Stalin deeply distrusted and feared each other. Stalin regarded Mao as a "national" Communist who placed Chinese interests above those of the Russians, and he feared that Mao could dilute his authority in the international Communist movement, particularly in Asia and the third world. Mao was deeply embittered by Stalin's repeated efforts to subvert Mao's leadership of the CCP and to substitute Chinese leaders who had been trained in Moscow. Because of his deep distrust of Stalin, it is reasonable to assume that Mao did not want to become overly dependent on the Soviet dictator.[2]

A second reason why Mao might have wanted normal relations with the United States in 1949 was his long expressed desire for American economic assistance to help rebuild China. As early as 1946, Mao told United States diplomat John Stewart Service that the United States was the *only* country capable of rendering postwar economic assistance to China in the amounts needed and that it was in the interests of both countries to have friendly relations.

A third factor to be borne in mind is the fact that the Chinese Communist leadership in 1949 was not monolithic. Some evidence suggests that the leadership was then divided into "nationalist" currents inclined to be suspicious of Moscow and "internationalist" currents inclined to greater loyalty to Moscow. Mao was consistently associated with the "nationalist" current. The first clash between "pro-Soviet" and "anti-Soviet" factions within the CCP came in Manchuria between 1946 and 1949 during the Chinese civil war. The leaders of the "anti-Soviet" faction at this time were P'eng Chen and Lin Feng. The "pro-Soviet" faction was led by Kao Kang and Li Li-san. The issues in conflict centered, first, around the proper military strategy to fight the civil war and, second, around the relationship between the Chinese leaders and the military officers and administrators from the Soviet Union who had moved into Manchuria in the closing days of World War II. In 1964, once Sino-Soviet polemics had erupted into the open, Moscow charged that P'eng and Lin had in this period "intentionally distorted the role of the Soviet army [in Manchuria] and disseminated slanders against the USSR." Moreover, said the Russians, instances of "anti-Soviet statements" in the "higher echelons" of the CCP became "so open" that by 1949 the Chinese Central Committee, apparently as a result of Soviet pressure, was forced to condemn the "mistakes" of the P'eng-Lin group.

Despite these strong criticisms by the Russians, both P'eng and Lin rose steadily under Mao in the CCP hierarchy after 1949 to positions of great prominence before they both became victims of the Cultural Revolution. The pro-Soviet Kao Kang, on the other hand, was swiftly purged by Mao immediately after Stalin's death.[3]

Finally, there is evidence to suggest that Mao would have

liked American recognition in 1949. According to Soviet documents, before making his "lean to one side" speech in 1949, Mao had actually expressed the view that it would be better if China were recognized first by the United States and other Western powers before being recognized by the Soviet Union.[4] And throughout most of 1949, the official Chinese media stressed China's desire for recognition without conditions by all outside powers. It was the United States that imposed several preconditions for recognition that the Chinese Communists were evidently not prepared to meet.

Thus, although ideological factors undoubtedly did play some role in helping to align China with Russia in 1949, considerations of national security were probably decisive. In the absence of any possibility for a normal relationship with the United States, and in view of the fact that the United States was increasingly coming to identify the Chinese Communists as part of a worldwide Communist monolith which needed to be contained, Peking had little alternative to a lopsided alliance with Moscow.

A second major turning point in Chinese foreign policy, the decision to break with Moscow in 1960, can also be explained largely on nondoctrinal grounds. The crucial turning point in Sino-Soviet relations came between 1957 and 1959. Two developments in this period were probably decisive. First, Moscow initially decided to enter into some sort of a nuclear sharing arrangement with Peking and then reneged, probably because it began to get cold feet about the prospect of a nuclear-armed China on its borders. Khrushchev tried to backtrack and to bring China under Soviet nuclear control, but when this effort failed, Moscow withdrew its nuclear assistance. Second, in the same period, Khrushchev launched the "spirit of Camp David," visited the United States, and sought to begin a detente with President Eisenhower. This event, coming as it did so soon after the nuclear controversy, must have convinced Mao that the Russians were prepared to sacrifice Chinese interests to the Americans. The offshore island crisis in 1958, in which the Russians refused to give much support to Peking until the crisis was past its peak, and Soviet neutrality in the Sino-Indian border conflict in 1959 were the last straws for Mao. When Khrushchev attempted to blackmail China into submission by pulling out all Soviet technicians and withdrawing Soviet economic assistance to China in 1960, the conflict became irreparable.

A third major turning point in Chinese foreign policy came in the 1960s when the Chinese began increasingly to support so-called "wars of national liberation" in the third world. The famous statement by Lin Piao in 1964 which outlined Peking's thinking on "people's war" was widely commented upon in the West.

Fortunately, a very thorough study of Chinese policy on "liberation wars" has been made by Peter Van Ness.[5] And, as Van Ness has conclusively demonstrated, China's support for revolutionary movements during the 1960s was highly selective. Contrary to widespread assumptions, Peking did not adopt a firm, across-the-board policy in support of "liberation" struggles everywhere. It supported some of these struggles and refused to support, or even to acknowledge, others. The primary consideration in Peking's decision whether to support armed struggles in the independent countries of Asia, Africa, and Latin America was the particular government's policy toward Peking. When governments were friendly to China, the Chinese did *not* support armed struggles against them. When governments were unfriendly to China, the Chinese did support such armed struggles. Usually, the unfriendly countries were pro-American. Thus, Peking had two very good reasons of national interest for supporting armed struggles against those governments. They were unfriendly to China and they were allied to China's main enemy at the time—the United States.

For a year or two, during the Cultural Revolution in 1966 and 1967, Peking did break with this selective approach to revolution-mongering. It began to adopt revolutionary tactics in countries where it had previously refrained from doing so. Thus, in 1966, Peking began to support antiregime movements in Burma, a country that had maintained a friendly attitude with China and in which Peking had for the most part refrained from supporting armed struggles. But as soon as the Cultural Revolution came to an end, Peking reverted swiftly to its earlier policy and sought to improve its relations with the Ne Win government in Rangoon while toning down its support for insurgency movements.

In sum, the Chinese were extremely selective in their support of armed struggles abroad. The policy was not one of spreading revolutions indiscriminately. It was a policy of supporting revolutionary movements against selected governments unfriendly to China.

A fourth critical foreign policy decision of the Peking government was the decision to enter into a rapprochement with the United States in the early 1970s. This decision, perhaps most clearly of all, was motivated by reasons of national security. Between 1965 and 1971, the Soviet Union tripled its ground forces on the Chinese border and equipped them with nuclear-armed missiles. In 1968, the Soviet Union invaded Czechoslovakia and enunciated a doctrine that sanctioned its right to intervene in the affairs of any dissident Communist state. In 1969, actual fighting broke out on the Sino-Soviet frontier along the Amur-Ussuri boundary. In seeking a rapprochement with its erstwhile major enemy, the United States, China was clearly pursuing classical balance-of-power tactics—aligning itself with one superpower in order to deter the other.

It is noteworthy, moreover, that Peking's fear of Soviet expansion has caused it to oppose the spread of revolutionary movements abroad wherever those movements may enhance the position of the Soviet Union. Thus, Peking provided aid to the two factions in the Angolan civil war that were opposed to the pro-Soviet MPLA. Peking has sent arms to the Mobutu government in Zaire that is being challenged by a Cuban and Soviet-backed force of Katangan gendarmes from Angola. In Oman, Peking withdrew its support from the Dhofar rebellion in order to curry favor with the anti-Soviet Shah of Iran. During the breakup of Pakistan in the early 1970s, Peking opposed a Bangladesh "liberation" movement led by self-proclaimed Maoists in order to back the government in West Pakistan, a government that was useful to Peking in opposing the spread of Indian and Soviet influence on the subcontinent.

Not only is China now downplaying, and in some cases actively opposing, revolutionary movements but it is earnestly courting the most anti-Soviet politicians it can find abroad. Thus, in recent years the guests of honor in Peking have been people such as Franz Joseph Strauss, former British conservative leader Edward Heath, former American defense secretary James Schlesinger, former American president Richard Nixon, and the outspokenly anti-Soviet conservative leaders of Australia and New Zealand. In the United States, Japan, and in Western Europe, the Chinese have deliberately cultivated the most anti-Soviet leaders and intellectuals that they could find.

Finally, Peking is now encouraging the continuation of a strong American military presence in the Pacific as a counterweight to the Russians. The Chinese have informed many Japanese politicians that they do not object to the continuation of the United States-Japan Security Treaty; they have hinted to President Marcos that they have no objections to the continuation of American bases in the Philippines; they support the ANZUS Pact that brings together Australia, New Zealand, and the United States in a military alliance; and Peking supports the new American base at Diego Garcia in the Indian Ocean.

In sum, one reason for doubting the central role of doctrine in explaining Peking's foreign policy since 1949 is the fact that most of the key foreign policy decisions made by the Chinese Communists can be satisfactorily explained on nondoctrinal grounds. In all four of the cases I have just explored, there were important considerations of security and interest involved.

But there are other reasons for doubting the centrality of doctrine as an explanatory variable for Chinese foreign policy. First, Chinese doctrine, like any doctrine, is compatible with alternative courses of action. I know of no key decision in foreign policy made by the Chinese Communists since 1949 that did not arouse controversy within the party.

In 1949, the leadership was divided between an "internationalist," pro-Soviet group led by Liu Shao ch'i that wanted to rely exclusively on an alliance with the Soviet Union and a more "nationalist" group led by Mao that wanted to balance between the Soviet Union and the Western powers. United States policy at the time precluded such an alternative. In the late 1950s and early 1960s, Mao's decision to break with Russia was opposed by some of the top military leaders, including the then Minister of Defense, P'eng Te-Huai. In the mid-1960s, during the Vietnam war, many Chinese leaders wanted to reach an accommodation with Moscow in order to oppose the United States in Vietnam, but such a compromise was vetoed by Mao. Subsequently, Mao's decision to seek an accommodation with the United States was evidently opposed by Lin Piao and other military leaders.

Thus, throughout the past twenty-five years, the Chinese leadership has often been divided on the most basic issues of foreign policy. It is therefore difficult to conclude that the doctrine of the Chinese Communist leaders dictates a specific course of action in foreign affairs.

A more modest argument may be made that although

Chinese Communist values cannot account for the *selection* of a particular foreign policy option, those values do limit the *range* of options open to the leadership. But even in this form, the argument is difficult to sustain. China has moved in the past twenty-five years from an exclusive alliance with the Soviet Union in the 1950s, to a policy of opposition to both superpowers in the 1960s, to a policy of "tilting" toward the United States in the 1970s. Thus China has already exercised virtually the entire range of options open to it in dealing with the two superpowers. It has allied with Russia against the United States; it has opposed both; and, more recently, it has come close to allying itself with the United States against Russia.

Second, any foreign policy decision can be justified on ideological grounds. Even a decision to ally temporarily with the "main enemy," such as the Soviet decision to sign the Nazi-Soviet pact and the Chinese decision to sign the Shanghai Communique, can always be justified on the grounds that there are greater dangers than those involved in temporary alliances. It is true that there have been signs of disagreement within the Chinese leadership over these decisions just as there was chaos throughout the entire international Communist movement when Stalin signed the pact with Hitler. But the decisions were made and they were justified on ideological grounds. Although this does not mean that ideology is irrelevant in explaining foreign policy, or that ideology should be treated as eyewash, it does suggest that ideology cannot be the central focus of explanation.

Third, a good case can be made that the Chinese Communists have consistently thought in balance-of-power terms ever since the 1930s when Mao first took control of the party. As the Chinese Communists themselves have pointed out, a crucial part of their "revolutionary" doctrine is the notion of a "united front" strategy. At any given historical moment, this strategy dictates the identification of the "main enemy" and the mobilizing of all available forces against him. A review of CCP history demonstrates that if there is any one key to Chinese Communist thinking, this classical balance-of-power approach is it.

Until the Japanese invasion of China in 1937, the main enemy of the CCP was Chiang Kai-shek, against whom the Communists sought to mobilize the broadest possible united front. After 1937, Japan became the main enemy, and the Communists cooperated with anyone who was willing to fight the Japanese, including Chiang and the Americans. Throughout the 1950s, China sought to mobilize the Communist bloc and whatever third-world forces it could find against American "imperialism." After the emergence of the Sino-Soviet split in the 1960s, China identified the Soviet Union as its main enemy and now seeks to mobilize whatever forces it can find against the Russians. In pursuing this policy, Peking has entered into a quasi-alliance with the United States, has cultivated the most anti-Soviet forces in Europe and Asia, and has called for the strengthening of NATO, the United States-Japan Security Treaty, and other such alliances.

Thus, throughout the past forty years, one can find a continuous thread running through Chinese Communist behavior. It has not been a doctrinal thread; rather, it constitutes extraordinary flexibility designed to rally a broad coalition of forces against whatever enemy the Chinese Communists single out as their main enemy of the day.

Let me conclude this essay with some qualifying remarks. In downgrading the value of "ideological" explanations of China's foreign policy, I am not adding my voice to those who simplistically dismiss ideology altogether as a mere rationalization of allegedly more fundamental considerations such as power and interest. I am aware that ideas and interests and ideas and power cannot be juxtaposed: They interact and shape each other. Nor do I argue that ideology is irrelevant. After all, men who have spent their entire adult lives fighting in the name of a revolutionary ideology can hardly be dismissed as Machiavellians.

What I am arguing is that, even in China, where revolutionary doctrine *is* still very much alive, where the revolution is not yet dead and buried, most of Chinese foreign policy decisions can be explained without reference to the doctrine. Moreover, the doctrine is broad enough to encompass an enormous range of alternative policies. Thus, although I do not doubt for a moment that ideology may have *some* explanatory value, it is not an independent variable in explaining Chinese foreign policy. A more important "key" to Chinese foreign policy lies in China's interaction with other states within the international community, particularly the great powers, and in its quest for traditional values like power, influence, and security. In dealing with China, our statesmen would thus be better off assuming that as far as foreign policy is concerned, China is a "normal" country.

NOTES

1. See my article, "Mao's Role in the Sino-Soviet Conflict," *Pacific Affairs,* Summer, 1974.

2. *Ibid.*

3. For the details, see the biographies of Kao Kang, Lin Feng, and P'eng Chen in Donald W. Klein and Anne B. Clark, *Biographic Dictionary of Chinese Communism, 1921-1965* (Cambridge, Mass., 1971).

4. O.B. Borisov and B.T. Koloskov, *Soviet-Chinese Relations, 1945-1970,* ed. Vladimir Petrov (Bloomington, Indiana, 1975), p. 122.

5. Peter Van Ness, *Revolution and Chinese Foreign Policy* (Berkeley, Calif., 1971).

8.

The Organic Relationship between Ideology and Political Reality
Hans J. Morgenthau

When one talks about ideology, especially with regard to foreign policy, one is in a situation not dissimilar to that in which one finds oneself when one uses terms like imperialism, communism, national liberation, and so forth. That is to say, underlying those concepts there are certain value judgments that in a negative or positive way predetermine one's position with regard to a particular foreign policy. When we talk about an ideology of foreign policy, we imply that what this ideology propounds is a mere pretense and is not to be taken seriously as a genuine reflection of reality. On the other hand, when we talk about a philosophy of foreign policy we assume that we are in the presence of a reflection of the true state of things. Discoursing on politics, domestic or international, one has to make what can be called a moral effort to look objectively at a certain situation, at the interplay between ideas, rationalizations, and justifications, on the one hand, and the empirical facts, on the other. I am using here the term ideology in an objective, sociological way, which has been most clearly and influentially defined by Karl Mannheim. I call an ideology, regardless of the motive or the state of mind of its propounder, any system of thought which rationalizes or justifies a particular social position.

117

Thus any philosophy that has an influence on the thinking and the attitudes of individuals has an ideological function within the social context in which it operates. I should also say that if there is merit in those distinctions that I have intimated, then any foreign policy, especially when it is of an even moderately civilized nature, is bound to be overlain by an ideology that intends to justify morally and rationalize intellectually that particular foreign policy. In other words, ideology is not a propagandistic addition to foreign policy. It is an intrinsic element within the foreign policy process itself. That this is so, that this is bound to be so, results from the very nature of politics and the ambivalent moral and rational position that individuals take toward politics. In order to make this clear, let me make a few elementary statements that support this assertion.

If it is true that the essence of politics is a competitive struggle for power, then the individual involved in the political process is bound to take an ambivalent position within that process. On the one hand, he is a potential master, the holder of political power, the seeker after power, which search is the very essence of his political activity. On the other hand, he is a potential object of the political power of others that he tries to fend off by being active within the political sphere. Thus the individual is both a potential holder of political power and a potential object of political power. This being so, the ambivalence of his existential position within the political process is bound to be reflected in his moral value judgments and his rational ruminations about politics. The ideologies that he develops are at the same time justifications and rationalizations of his drive for power and rationalizations and justifications of his defensive attitude toward the power of others.

Furthermore, in order for the struggle for power to be effective for one or the other or both sides, it is necessary, you may even say it is essential, for these aspirations for power on the part of A vis-à-vis B to appear as something different from what they actually are. For if A enters the arena of political combat with the open declaration "I want power over B," he will alert B and the friends of B and may well discourage his own potential friends who are afraid of his power. If he is able to conceal the actual essence of his aspirations in the political arena by political ideologies, if he can make it appear that what he wants is not primarily power over B but something else, such as the common good or the realization of some other objective value to which most or all members of this particular segment of society can adhere, then he has already won one battle in the political combat. He has already half disarmed his opponents and the prospective objects of his power and weakened their resistance by making it appear that what he wants is something else but power and that for this reason there is no moral or rational justification for opposing him. In order to appreciate the pervasive need for ideologies, one has only to look at the cant with which the struggle for power is concealed, however thinly, in our periodic election campaigns and how fatal it is for a prospective competitor in those campaigns to come out openly and say what he wants is power or, if he wants to be president, to admit that what he wants is the supreme power in the land. It is fatal for a candidate for political office to admit that he is resolved to gain this office at almost any price. What he has to do is the exact opposite: to make it appear that he is really not terribly interested in this office per se; but he is a patriot, he has certain moral principles by which he abides, he has a political program that he wants to see enacted, and he cannot disappoint the people who expect his services. Thus the point I want to make is that ideological justifications and rationalizations are not arbitrary decorations of the political scene, they are not accidental accretions to the essence of the political struggle, they are organic elements of that struggle itself.

Now let me say a word about the ideologies of American foreign policy. From what I have said it must be obvious that American foreign policy partakes, as do all foreign policies, of this organic relationship to ideologies. That is to say, American foreign policy, from the very beginning of American history, has been justified and rationalized by ideologies. Take, for example, the most typical American ideology of American foreign policy: Manifest Destiny. The historic fact that the triumphant westward expansion of American power was the result of an extreme discrepancy of power between the native Indians and the pioneer settlers was concealed by a quasi-theological conception to the effect that providence had reserved the North American continent to pioneer settlement. The geographic limits of that Manifest Destiny have changed both with the opportunity and with the preferences of the propounders of the doctrine. There were people in the United States, during the nineteenth century, particularly clergymen, who maintained that the whole western hemisphere from the north to the south pole was reserved by divinity to the American settlers. There have been more modest writers who had a divine inspiration to the effect that it was only the North American continent, with or without Canada, that was thus reserved. But the connection between the counsels of providence and the ultimate goal of American policy was firmly established in the minds and in the utterances of American public men in the nineteenth century.

I should say in passing that this connection is of course intimately related to another ideology, another basic conception suggested to Americans by the very nature of American history and by the very relations that the United States was able to maintain with other nations, at least up to the Spanish-American War. It was the conviction that American foreign policy is not subject to the same kinds of moral risks and political and intellectual temptations to which the foreign policies of other nations are subject. In other words, the activities of Americans on the chessboard of foreign policy are endowed with a particular virtue absent from the foreign policies of other nations. American foreign policy has proceeded not by way of egotistic aspirations or, as one would say today, imperialistic aspirations and policies, but by way of policies that were at least intended to be beneficial to all concerned and, more particularly, to the objects of American foreign policy.

The classic example of this substitution of an ideology for the facts of political life is the utterance of Senator Beveridge of Indiana in 1899 on the occasion of the debate in the Senate concerning the annexation of the Philippines. The senator justified the annexation by stating that we have to bring the blessings of Christian civilization to our little brown brothers for whom Christ also died. The problem of sugar, for instance, did not appear in those justifications and rationalizations. Nor did the geopolitical importance of the Philippines for American strategy. What appeared was a very thick layer of ideological concealments and justifications that was in a particular way pleasing and flattering to the self-understanding of Americans as a nation among nations.

Americans have viewed their participation in the Spanish-American War and in the two world wars not as selfish moves on behalf of certain concrete interests, as was the case of the Soviet Union at the end of the Second World War. Rather they looked at it as an almost humanitarian intervention for the purpose of preventing certain wrongs from being committed and of righting certain wrongs already committed. This is another aspect of the same self-delusion resulting from ideological rationalizations and justifications that has been extremely important in instrumental terms for the rallying of American public opinion in support of those wars. One can go one step farther and say that when this identification of American purposes in foreign policy with certain objective moral and rational values was no longer plausible, as it ceased to be after the first and second world wars, another ideology had to be furnished to justify the disappointment, the disillusionment, and the abstentionist if not isolationist mental attitude following therefrom.

A classic example of this situation is the Vietnam War. If one looks at the justifications of that war, one realizes that they follow the same pattern of allegedly unselfish humanitarian purposes by which the other military interventions of the United States at least since the beginning of the century were rationalized and justified. That is to say, as in the first and second world wars, we did not pursue in Vietnam any specific advantages of the traditional strategic, economic, or political kind. What we wanted was not, to quote Woodrow Wilson, to restore the balance of power that had been disturbed in August 1914 but to put an end to that pernicious system of international relations and to substitute a consortium of power for the traditional balance. In the same way, we waged the Second World War not for the purpose of annexing some territory, or of substituting American power for somebody else's power, or of becoming the most powerful nation on earth but in order to wipe off the face of the earth that unspeakable evil called nazism.

The rationalizations and justifications of the Vietnam War are echoes of those ideologies with which the preceding American wars were justified. The only difference is that the ideological letdown that followed the two world wars coincided with our fighting the Vietnam War. That is to say, the plausibility of the ideological justifications and rationalizations concerning that war did not survive its reality. In good measure, I would guess, the impact of modern communications was responsible for this ideological collapse, aside from the intrinsic implausibility of that war in terms of the ideological tradition of America.

Finally, and perhaps most importantly, an ideology does not survive confrontation with a reality that denies it. Although the victories in the two world wars at least provided seeming support for the ideologies with which those wars were fought, the impossibility of making sense of the Vietnam War or of even coming close to winning it cast a shadow of doubt if not a clear denial upon the ideologies with which that war was rationalized and justified. Thus if one considers the history of American ideologies of foreign policy, one finds an intimate relationship between those ideologies and the very conception Americans have had of their own individuality, of their own specific national character, against the individuality and the national character of other nations. That is to say, the ideologies of a particular virtue, especially in terms of unselfishness, of a particular providential guidance or design, are not arbitrary additions to a propagandistic effort. Rather they grow out organically from the very conception Americans have formed of who they are and what they are all about in their relations with other nations.

9.

Ideology and Foreign Policy: The American Experience
Arthur M. Schlesinger, jr.

Our concern in this discussion, I take it, is with the connection between words and deeds in the conduct of foreign affairs. We may well begin by looking first at the question of behavior—what governments do—before moving on to the question of ideology—what governments think and/or say about why they do it.

Let me indicate my own approach by confessing agreement with what George Washington called in 1778 "a maxim founded on the universal experience of mankind, that no nation is to be trusted farther than it is bound by its interest." Washington was not predicting that nations always act in terms of their interests. Rather he was saying that, without the magnetic compass of national interest, there could be no regularity or predictability, and therefore no intelligible order, in international affairs. He was also suggesting that, among the several obligations of nationhood, the supreme obligation must be the survival of its people. If this is so, nations plainly have no choice but to act in terms of power.

Yet, if nations must *act* in terms of power, it does not necessarily follow that they will *think* in terms of power, and it certainly does not follow thay they will *talk* in terms of power. National interest is an elusive enough concept in itself. However defined, it rarely remains free of the taint of ideology. What then is the relationship between ideology and national interest? Is ideology simply the one-to-one projection of somebody's idea of national interest? Or is it a semi-dependent variable that affects the definition of the national interest? Or is it an independent variable that on occasion may cause nations to take actions against their national interest?

In American history ideology does not imply an explicit, comprehensive, metahistorical theology, a body of revealed truth, like Leninism or Hitlerism. Americans have had little penchant for ideology in the grand manner. Instead we have had a laundry list of vague and benign purposes. This is partly because we have not been temperamentally disposed to reduce the bracing diversity of history to a single all-encompassing code. It is also partly because, even if we were so disposed, we have lacked a single party, like the Communists or Nazis, capable of promulgating and enforcing such a code.

That laundry list of benign purposes is not, I must add, inconsiderable simply because it does not constitute an integrated and dogmatic revelation. There is certainly, as Gunnar Myrdal suggested thirty years ago, an American creed. Myrdal defined that creed as embracing the ideas of the essential dignity of the individual human being, of the fundamental equality of all persons, and of certain inalienable rights to freedom, justice, and fair opportunity. The tension between the American creed and the American reality creates the American Dilemma; and, as Myrdal emphasized, that tension has been a major source of American social progress.[1] The discrepancy between the ideal and the actuality and the desire to bring the actuality up toward the ideal has been the great instigating and legitimating factor in the whole history of American reform.

But the American creed is highly general. It does not prescribe foreign policy as *Mein Kampf* did, or as the works of

Lenin and Stalin did. It bears upon foreign policy insofar as it delineates values that govern definitions of the national interest. But it cannot determine in any very specific way the content of foreign policy.The Founding Fathers, for example, thought that America had a mission to the world. But, in their view, if America was to redeem the world, it was as a model, not as a master. They did not construe the American mission as that of going abroad, in the famous words of John Quincy Adams, "in search of monsters to destroy." It was by our example that we might hope to regenerate mankind, not by our intervention. In recent times, however, we have come to construe the American creed as requiring our direct entry into the inner lives of foreign countries in order to straighten out lesser breeds and set them on the road to salvation. In this context ideology would appear a form of rationalization. In the first half century of the republic, ideology rationalized the impotence of a weak state whose only conceivable hope of influencing the world was by example. In our own time the ideology of intervention may well rationalize the overweening power of a mighty state.

The concept, I have said, is elusive. Twenty-five years ago George Kennan, in *American Diplomacy, 1900-1950,* set forth an impressive and influential critique of American foreign policy. The American illusion, he suggested, was that legalistic and moralistic considerations should determine foreign policy decisions. His critique had considerable literary persuasiveness. Yet one wondered in what particular ways our foreign policy would have been different had it renounced the legalism and moralism to which Kennan so rightly objected. Was, indeed, this compound of legalism and moralism much more than the rhetoric in which abiding motives of foreign policy were concealed from the public and even, on occasion, from some of the actors themselves, as no doubt in the case of Wilson? It can be reasonably argued, I think, that in the first half of the twentieth century, the great foreign policy decisions, although expounded and defended in terms of law and morality, were taken in terms of power. Surely we entered both world wars, for example, not to make the world safe for democracy in 1917 or for the Four Freedoms in 1941, but for the reason that Thomas Jefferson had given in 1814—a reason controlling then and, I believe, still controlling today—that it would be an intolerable threat to the safety of the United States if "the whole force of Europe [were to be] wielded by a single hand." This was the concern that in earlier centuries had led to American participation in every European war with major naval operations in the North Atlantic and that in the later twentieth century would lead to American resistance to the Stalinization of Western Europe.

Ironically, Kennan's critique worked better as prophecy than as history. Although I do not believe that the ideological component in United States foreign policy had all that significant an influence in the first half of the twentieth century, it began to play a most destructive part in the years after Kennan's period (1900-1950) came to an end.

The United States, I suppose, entered the postwar world with two leading convictions about its international role: the conviction that the United States had an obligation to create and defend a global structure of peace; and the conviction that the United States had a democratizing mission to the world. I suppose these can be considered ideological convictions. I would even say that they were perfectly honorable convictions. But the pressures and temptations of the postwar situation led to the catastrophic overextension and misapplication of initially valid principles, a process that culminated horribly in the Indochina tragedy.

The foreign policy of the United States since the Second World War has been in the hands of the generation that reached maturity between 1914, the start of the First World War, and 1953, the end of the Korean War. Every generation is the prisoner of its own experience. And for that generation the critical international experience was the defense of the "peace system" against one or another aggressive power. Peace, it was said in the cliché of the time, was indivisible; appeasement only encouraged aggression; aggression anywhere, if unchecked and unpunished, threatened the independence of nations everywhere; the preservation of peace therefore required the reestablishment of the peace system through collective action against aggression by the world community. This was the view of the world—the ideology, if you like—envisaged by Woodrow Wilson; the view implied by the Stimson Doctrine; the view presumably substantiated by the failure of appeasement at Munich; the view argued by President Roosevelt during the Second World War; the view reasserted in the Truman Doctrine.

Obviously, something had gone badly wrong with the application of that doctrine by the time of Vietnam. Some would date the degeneration of the collective security idea with the Truman Doctrine of 1947—and in a sense this may be so, although I would emphasize *in a sense,* because inflation in the Truman period was in words, not in deeds. Truman formulated the Truman Doctrine in open-ended language but executed it very sparingly at the start. After supervising the greatest demobilization in American history, he kept defense spending for some time under tight control. In 1947-1950 our national security expenditures averaged $13 billion a year. The Korean War changed all that. But it was not till the 1950s that the United States government began to live by the spacious rhetoric of the Truman Doctrine.

The original collective security idea had been that clearcut acts of aggression by major states required intervention by the international community to restore a pre-existing balance of power. In the fifties, this idea lost its limitations. It was subtly transformed by Dulles and Eisenhower into the more problematic doctrine that almost any form of foreign trouble, whether caused by large or small states, whether the underlying elements of a balance-of-power situation existed, whether the trouble was external or internal in origin, required intervention, if necessary, by America alone. And so in the fifties the idea became charged with a righteous moralism that encouraged the American people to construe political questions in ethical terms, local questions in global terms, relative questions in absolute terms. In this messianic spirit, we abandoned any realistic assessment of our stakes in Southeast Asia. Nothing was more distressing in the Pentagon Papers than the apparent failure of any administration to recalculate the exact nature of our interest in Indochina, to consider in hard fact what the consequences would be for the United States of the communization of Indochina.

This misapplication of the doctrine of collective security was paralleled by the overapplication of the idea of America's regenerative mission to suffering mankind. Like collective security, this was in its original form a valuable idea. But in its original form, we have noted, the mission was to reform the world by American example, not by Americans moving into other countries and fixing things up themselves. Then the experience of military occupation after the Second World War—and especially, I think, the occupation of Japan—began to strengthen American confidence in our supposed talent for what we began to call "nation building." We soon supposed that we had not only the power but the wisdom to enter alien cultures and to reconstruct them according to our own standards and values. Under a kind of *mission civilatrice* of our own, we indulged in another fatal perversion of a sound idea. We were beguiled into what might be called sentimental imperialism: the belief that *we* knew better than other people did what was good for *them*.

In this process, the limited policy of helping others to help themselves grew into the unlimited policy of imposing our own preferences on others. So that if the Vietnamese would not, out of respect for our superior wisdom, do what we thought was good for them, we were determined to make them do it out of obedience to our superior strength. The Army major, standing in the rubble of Ben Tre, summed up the logic of American messianism when he said that it had become necessary to destroy the town to save it.

The ideological delusion that the United States was the appointed protector of world freedom received additional impetus from the conviction that world freedom was threatened by the centralized movement of world communism. Communism of the forties, which, for purposes of precision, we should call Stalinism, was of course not only a cruel tyranny in Soviet Russia but also a relatively coordinated international movement. In that period anti-Stalinism was surely a moral necessity for any believer in democracy. And, in that period, Stalinism was a perfectly genuine threat in Western Europe, not in the sense that the Red Army was going to invade, but in the sense that economic and social disorganization might have brought Stalinist parties to power. Unfortunately, the idea of practical resistance to the Stalinization of specific countries was soon absorbed in the cosmic proposition that communism was a changeless, unalterable, monolithic doctrine of total control and total evil. Again a rational idea underwent fatal expansion and perversion.

I would suggest that the recent debacle of American foreign policy has been a manifest result of distorted ideology. The reasonable conduct of foreign affairs withers away when ideology triumphs over a realistic concept of the national interest. It was surely no coincidence that the most powerful proponents of the realistic analysis of America's foreign policy, Hans Morgenthau, Walter Lippmann, Reinhold Niebuhr, and George Kennan, were all early and penetrating critics of American involvement in the war in Vietnam.

I suppose one further question remains. We have discussed ideology thus far as the official explanation of the aims of foreign policy. There is another problem with regard to ideology. That is the role of ideology in the interpretation of American foreign policy, by which I mean ideology as imputed by historians to those in government who make vital foreign policy decisions. There has arisen in recent times, for example, an influential historical school that explains American foreign policy as a remorseless exercise in expansionism, dictated by the internal needs of a capitalist system that must grow in order to survive, directed toward the establishment of a world economic hegemony under American control.

There are many specific difficulties with the application of this argument, but there is also a general difficulty, cogently argued, it seems to me, by Max Weber in his discussion of imperialism. Weber proposed that we make the mental experiment of assuming that all modern nation states were state-socialist communities; that is, associations supplying a maximum amount of their needs through a collective economy. The problem of imperialism, Weber said, would not change fundamentally if that assumption were made. A collective economy would be no less determined than would a free-market economy to procure as cheaply as possible indispensable goods not produced in its own territory. It is probable that force would be used where it would improve the conditions of exchange. "One cannot see why," Weber wrote, "the strong state-socialist communities should disdain to squeeze tribute out of the weaker communities . . . where they could do so."[2] Of course, the record of the Soviet Union in dominating, exploiting, and looting weaker states abundantly confirms Weber's analysis.

Following Weber, let us suppose that the United States never had that capitalist marketplace that is supposed to be the root of all empire, but that it had always been a Communist state, like the Soviet Union. Would a Communist United States have been any less inclined to expand across the North American continent? Would a Communist United States have been any happier to allow Spain, France, Great Britain, Germany, and Russia to occupy strategic points in the Western hemisphere or by the surrounding oceans? Would a Communist United States have refrained from dominating and exploiting the weaker states in Latin America? Would a Communist United States have failed to react against, say, the installation of nuclear missiles in Cuba by an anti-Communist power from across the seas? Would not a Communist United States be as determined as a capitalist United States to take the measures it deemed necessary to protect its national security?

It is hard, looking at modern history, to see imperialism as a specifically capitalist phenomenon. It is evidently a pervading fallacy to ascribe to economic reasons what can in most cases more persuasively be seen as *raisons d'etat.* In saying this, I would not exclude the possibility that the realist school, the school of national interest of which I am, I suppose, a fellow-traveler, may be committing an ideology of its own. I would simply conclude by suggesting that the relationship between words and deeds is as difficult to pin down in the actions of a government as it is in the actions of an individual. We all know how hard it is to determine when we as individuals express true motives or engage in rationalization and fakery. This may well be equally true in the conduct of states. So I will simply end by pleading that we extend the same tolerance and understanding to the motives by which governments behave as we would wish for ourselves.

NOTES

1. Gunnar Myrdal, *An American Dilemma* (New York, 1944), ch. 1.
2. H. H. Gerth and C. Wright Mills, *From Max Weber: Essays in Sociology* (New York, 1946), p. 169.

10.

Ideology and American Foreign Policy
Lloyd C. Gardner

During World War II experts in the North America section of the British Foreign Office puzzled for a time over what trends to expect in postwar United States foreign policy. Would it be dominated by the mentality displayed in Henry Luce's already famous *American Century,* or, alternatively, would it resemble that advocated in Henry Wallace's *Century of the Common Man*? Their conclusion, from the standpoint of British interests, was that the result would be about the same whichever Henry prevailed. Whether motivated by an assertive nationalism or by a dedicated internationalism, American policies were likely to conflict with traditional British (and European) prerogatives and plans.

What really worried British planners, however, was not the threat of American expansion. Quite the opposite, Professor H. G. Nicholas recalled of his days in the British embassy in Washington: The main concern expressed then was that the United States should not go back to what some had called the imperial isolationism of the years between the wars. It was very important for the world that the United States accept political responsibility for the consequences of its own acts and until the rest of mankind recovered from the war, for those of other nations as well.[1]

Another earlier generation of British statesmen had hoped that their American cousins would come to accept their full share of the "world's work." Joseph Chamberlain sincerely meant the congratulations that he extended to John Hay and Theodore Roosevelt in 1902 on the successful subduing of the Philippines. The colonial secretary wrote: "This extension of American influence and dominion will work for the happiness of the native population." He predicted that "the experience in the problems of government under such circumstances will help the American people to understand our world-work, and I hope to sympathize with it."[2] Cecil Rhodes believed that he was educating future generations of the American elite to understand and sympathize with the British Empire and to shape their thoughts about issues of concern to both nations by endowing the scholarship program that bore his name.

The "trustee" mentality of the late nineteenth century imperialists, which reached its peak at the Versailles conference, did not have much appeal for those Americans who resisted every effort to bring their country closer to European ideas. Woodrow Wilson's close adviser, Colonel Edward House, did conceive of a kind of informal understanding among industrial powers to develop the economies of the "backward" and "waste" places of the earth. But by 1916 both House and Wilson suspected that there would be difficulties with the Allies over America's war aims if it became necessary for the United States to go to war. Subsequently Wilson regretted the defeat of the League of Nations in the Senate not because he wanted to subordinate America to Europe, as his opponents charged, but because he believed that the only way to overcome the mistakes that Europe had made in the past was through American leadership. On his return from Paris in 1919, Wilson told an audience of supporters that the League of Nations was closely related to Washington's "utterance about entangling alliances. . . . And the thing that [Washington] . . . longed for was just what we are about to supply: an arrangement which will disentangle all the alliances in the world."³

Wilson shared the disenchantment that Americans suffered in the 1920s, and it would be a mistake to assume that American foreign policy followed the election returns. It would be equally mistaken to assume that either Republicans or Democrats, but not both, expressed the true character of the nation in foreign policy. Joseph Chamberlain's son, Austen, was responsible for the conduct of British foreign policy throughout much of the decade, and his lament applied equally to Wilson as well as to his three Republican successors:

> Apparently nothing will cure the Americans of the view that they are a people apart morally as well as geographically and that our policy is dictated by selfish motives and an overbearing temper which have no counterpart in the United States. We must accept these things as we find them, admit the unsurpassable barrier which exists to any effective cooperation and do that as we pay our debt . . . without whining. But I find it a little hard to stomach their constant dislike of being seen walking down the street with us even when they are profiting by what we do.⁴

The propensity to identify the American cause with the cause of civilization has, of course, been the subject of so much scholarly attention (as well as less informed criticism) that we need hardly draw attention to it here except to note a curious aspect of this reexamination of national motives and aspirations. Almost eager to accept foreign estimates of American policy that stress "idealism" or "moralism" as our guiding principles, we have, by and large, skipped over most of the harder questions associated with the problem of ideology. Thus we err—if indeed we do err—because of our robust naiveté, a crusading fervor carried to excess because, well, Americans do all things in excess. We even neglect national interests for this reason. And sometimes we are slow to

awaken to real peril because we retreat into isolation whenever things do not go our way. Indeed, some students of
American history were concerned lest a defeat in Vietnam
lead to a general repudiation of the nation's international
commitments.

The pendulum-swing interpretation of American history
and foreign policy rests largely upon such an analysis: an
excess of zeal followed by a dramatic swoop backward, liberalism then conservatism, idealism then narrow nationalism.
Recent polls find that Americans do profess a much greater
degree of belief in religion than do Europeans. Henry Luce
himself was a product of American "missionary" interest in
China, his parents having spent many years in answering the
call to a higher duty. Perhaps what Robert Altman and others
have been telling us recently is that the proper subtitle for a
book called *USA*, should be *Permanent Revival Meeting.*

Even so, it sometimes seems that we are in danger of discussing "motivation" when we think we are discussing ideology. Henry James talked about a paradox of a similar nature
at the turn of the century when he referred to the American
woman abroad, who "with her freedoms, her immunity from
traditions . . . represents the conservative element among a
cluster of persons. . . ."[5] One thinks also of President Ford's
survey of his accomplishments in foreign policy. The United
States, he said, had saved Portugal for democracy; and if the
Democrats in Congress had not faltered at the critical moment, we would have secured freedom for Portugal's un-
happy colony, Angola. The desire to bestow self-determination on others is almost a contradiction in terms. It goes back
to 1776, not to the Declaration of Independence but to the
clause in the Articles of Confederation that reserved a place
for Canada in the new union.

American motives for desiring Canadian inclusion involved
both strategic and ideological considerations. There was real
fear of attack, but ideology played a large part in determining

policy. Petitions were sent from the Continental Congress to other units in the Empire—Canada as well as Ireland and Jamaica. If they would join the revolt, how much easier it would be to justify a declaration of independence. Well aware that they would not be welcome ideologically amid a world of monarchies and mercantilistic empires, the leaders of the first new nation reached out for colonial reassurance as well as for foreign arms.

The ideological thrust of American policy in those first years of independence was so powerful (it had to be, perhaps, to compensate for material weakness) that it is not unfair to say that from 1776 to 1783 Americans behaved as if they were sure that they could adjust reality to their ideas only to find instead that they had to adjust their ideas to reality, at least temporarily, in order to survive.

The history of Canadian-American relations over the next century reflects a continuing need for ideological self-justification perhaps even more than "landhunger" or "annexation through reciprocity." Americans resented the Canadian failure to leave the British Empire; it gnawed at them, diminished their achievement, eluded their logic. James Madison launched invasion attempts in the War of 1812. Canadian willingness to join the United States had not become evident by the Civil War when William H. Seward suggested sending agents into British North America to stimulate independence movements. Senator Charles Sumner took up the quest with a post-Civil War demand that Great Britain yield Canada as payment for the *Alabama* claims. When London eventually met Canadian demands for self-government, the Maine state legislature declared the British North America Act of 1867 a violation of the Monroe Doctrine![6] Even as late as 1940, when some consideration was given to a plan for reestablishing the seat of the British government in Ottawa if Germany invaded the home isles, President Roosevelt was concerned about the adverse impact of reintroducing a monarchy anywhere in the hemisphere.

This review of Canadian-American relations should not be taken as a suggestion that man lives by ideology alone. Far from it. What is implied, rather, is that Americans considered their revolution to be an on-going struggle against the "old world" and its grip on the marketplace of ideas and goods. Victories in one realm, the ideological, were considered important to success in the other.

It was difficult, for example, for Thomas Jefferson, on returning from France to become secretary of state in the first Washington Administration, not to believe that the adjustments that his countrymen had made to reality were betrayals of the American Revolution. He had just left what he believed to be the beginning of a revolution stimulated by the American example. To turn one's back on the French Revolution thus became to Jefferson, and to those who thought like him, turning it on the American Revolution. All the table talk in Washington's inner circle, notes Julian Boyd, was about law and order—talk that was profoundly distressing to the author of the Declaration of Independence.

Jefferson feared a return to monarchical principles and mercantilism more than the threat of a return of the British monarch. It was not a long step logically to the conclusion that the presence of alien systems of government on the North American continent endangered liberty. We would do well to look into the expansionist thrust of the American Revolution with the same care historians have exercised in examining French revolutionary expansionism. Jefferson and his intellectual heirs had very little difficulty in rationalizing a strong forward movement against the Spanish possessions in North America and in even looking ahead to the time when the whole hemisphere would share the same language and political forms. As he put it in an 1801 letter to James Monroe, ". . .[Nor] can we contemplate with satisfaction either blot or mixture on that surface."[7]

Whatever doubts Jefferson may have had about territorial expansion beyond the Mississippi, he was committed to the idea that the American Revolution would never stop spreading. When the French Revolution did not develop as he had anticipated, Jefferson was disappointed but not discouraged. Toward the end of the nineteenth century, however, many Americans began to feel that a new danger from Europe threatened their well-being and political stability. Woodrow Wilson chose his words carefully in an address marking the nation's first hundred years under the Constitution:

> For us this is the centennial year of Washington's inauguration; but for Europe it is the centennial year of the French Revolution. One hundred years ago we gained, and Europe lost, self-command, self-possession. But since then we have been steadily receiving into our midst and to full participation in our national life the very people whom their home politics have familiarized with revolution: our own equable blood we have suffered to receive into it the most feverish blood of the restless old world.[8]

What Wilson seemed to be saying was that European radicalism from the time of the French Revolution was in reality reactionary, out of place in the "new" world. Like others alarmed about recent waves of immigration, Wilson was obviously worried about a kind of subversion. Before World War I, Americans did not think of their politics as "left" or "right." Such terms had a meaning only in the European context. The few manifestations of radical politics in the United States were damned as "anarchism," a rubric that covered everything one needed to say about such outbursts and carried the connotation of reactionary or precivilized. In World War I, despite the results of the Spanish-American War, Americans still considered themselves anticolonialists. Wilson projected the League of Nations as a remedy for European errors, as a recreation of the world in the image of the American Revolution.

The supreme irony that helped to undo Wilson was his faith in Russia—a fit partner for a League of Honor as he described the Provisional Government—working with him to correct the mistakes of the past. Not only was that hope dashed but Wilson's frustration at the Bolshevik triumph became all the worse because it forced him to deal with a man like Clemenceau. For his own purposes Lenin had seized on the non-Marxist principle of self-determination and made it a weapon against the Allied intervention. Wilson was caught: He could not pursue American war aims without seeming to support Lenin; he could not abandon them without seeming to yield to Anglo-French domination. The series of compromises that the president accepted at Versailles cannot, of course, be ascribed to the Bolshevik dilemma. There were plenty of reasons for his postwar difficulties in dealing with European leaders, but he had counted on having the ideological initiative. Lenin deprived him of that leverage.

The world was not yet ready to be recreated in the image of the American Revolution. Very well, then, we would not seek to provide political leadership for nations unwilling to see the folly of their ways. (It was the Senate, of course, that had rejected the Treaty of Versailles.) But the willingness of the United States to engage other world powers in conferences on specific questions suggests not an "isolationist" preoccupation so much as a desire to apply American economic power and influence where they would do the most good. Wilsonians doubted that that would be enough to prevent a recurrence of war, although even many committed internationalists looked back on the decision to stay out of the League of Nations as less important than it had seemed at the time. Moreover, working outside the League had certain advantages. The United States was not hampered, for example, in proposing solutions to the German reparations problem, as it might have been if it had had to take into account obligations under the Treaty of Versailles.

War did come again and with it a resurgence of ideological concern. American leaders sighed with relief when Russia seemed willing to give assurances that it would behave as a traditional national state after the war. Franklin Roosevelt even recruited "Uncle Joe" Stalin for his anticolonial team to oppose the British and French in the expected postwar contest over empire. Much to Churchill's chagrin, FDR talked openly about Russian and Chinese support for his plan to take Indochina, for example, away from the French. At last Russia would play the role that Woodrow Wilson had hoped it would play at Versailles.

During the Cold War conservative commentators pilloried Roosevelt's ghost for this naiveté and were even more harsh in condemning the supposed "liberal" notion that Mao's legions were nothing more than "agrarian reformers." Nevertheless, there remained (through all the name-calling and McCarthyite degradation) a widespread belief that the American Revolution and American "know-how" could demonstrate more appeal and generate more enthusiasm in the third world if freed from European influences than could communism.

In this sense, John Foster Dulles's quest for a George Washington for South Vietnam was neither the product of a moralizing self-righteousness nor the end result of Wilsonian idealism that many liberal and realist critics charged. Dulles was solidly within the American tradition in foreign policy. Roosevelt never lived to carry out his promise to end French rule in Indochina nor did Dulles succeed in preventing a "Communist takeover" after the French were finally defeated. But Graham Greene's quiet American did become the foster son and heir presumptive of Henry James's American woman who had invaded the quiet parlors of the European aristocracy with such devastating results for the entire world.

Vietnam did not prove that Americans no longer had the will to uphold their ideology or to meet their commitments.

Like the war of the Revolution itself, which then became only the nation's second longest war, Vietnam turned out to be a time that tried men's souls. From the time of the American Revolution to World War I, history and American ideology seemed to be moving in the same direction. The United States was then, at least morally, on the side of what Arno Mayer has called the forces of motion as opposed to the forces of position or order. With the postwar era and the Cold War, however, we entered a period in which the values and advantages of our revolution suffered a decreasing appeal to other areas of the world.

Lyndon Johnson eventually found that the Cold War consensus had disappeared. The nation had divided, but in doing so Americans initiated a serious dialogue (if they took the opportunity) about whether motivation could really guarantee a favorable reception for the American Revolution in 1976 any more than it had in 1776.

NOTES

1. Interview with H.G. Nicholas, February 17, 1974.
2. Quoted in Howard K. Beale, *Theodore Roosevelt and the Rise of America to World Power* (Baltimore, 1956), pp. 148-149.
3. Speech of March 4, 1919, from a copy in, *The Papers of Woodrow Wilson,* Library of Congress, Washington, D.C.
4. Austen Chamberlain to Sir Esme Howard, May 9, 1927, *The Papers of Austen Chamberlain,* Birmingham University Library, Birmingham, England.
5. This paradoxical theme runs through many of James's novels, but the quotation is from *The Portrait of a Lady.*
6. See Charles S. Campbell, *The Transformation of American Foreign Relations, 1865-1900* (New York, 1976), chs. 1 and 2
7. *The Writings of Thomas Jefferson,* Paul Leicester Ford, ed., 10 vols. (New York, 1892-99), VIII, 105.
8. Wilson's speech is reprinted in, Lloyd C. Gardner, ed., *A Different Frontier* (Chicago, 1966), p. 55.

11.

Ideology: Reality or Rhetoric?
George Schwab

From the preceding contributions it is clear why states that are underpinned by a basically secular or nonideological notion of politics have been omitted from consideration, even though they do from time to time invoke certain universal concepts to degrade actual or potential adversaries. The United States, however, was not excluded from consideration because it is supposed by many that its foreign policy vis-à-vis sovereign states has quite consistently reflected certain ideas that are often referred to as ideological. As its foreign policy has, however, never approached the scope of truly ideologically inspired political powers, namely, those of totalitarian one-party states, and in view of the fact that from the perspective of ideas it has supposedly often transcended the largely secular or nonideological states, it can perhaps be argued that the United States occupies an intermediate position between such states, on the one hand, and totalitarian one-party states, on the other hand.

In contrast to totalitarian one-party states whose *Weltanschauungen* are absolute and all-embracing and whose intentions are to remodel the world according to the particular worldview propounded, the United States, as Arthur Schlesinger, jr. has correctly observed, does not "prescribe foreign policy as *Mein Kampf* did, or as the works of Lenin and Stalin did." This qualitative difference between totalitarian one-party states and the United States can be attributed to the deeply ingrained belief of the American people in the virtues of political liberalism and cultural pluralism.

Although the United States has quite consistently arrogated to itself universal concepts such as humanity, justice, and progress, it is precisely because of this difference that the United States has never translated these concepts into militant doctrines of action. The lack of a coherently worked out set of ideas, an all-embracing *Weltanschauung* of a global scope, and the absence therefore of a party machinery to implement the ideology propounded, is the reason why, for example, the United States has never been in the position to challenge what Karl Mannheim has referred to as the "opponent's total *Weltanschauung*,"[1] a characteristic intrinsic to totalitarian one-party states. At the very most, one can argue that the quite consistent arrogation by the United States of certain universal concepts—the so-called ideologcal posture of the United States—conforms to an extent to what Mannheim has referred to as the "particular conception of ideology." According to him this conception

> makes its analysis of ideas on a purely psychological level. If it is claimed for instance that an adversary is lying, or that he is concealing or distorting a given factual situation, it is still nevertheless assumed that both parties share common criteria of validity—it is still assumed that it is possible to refute and eradicate sources of error by referring to accepted criteria of objective validity common to both parties.[2]

Of course, this posture presupposes two or more fundamentally hostile systems coexisting in a condition of mutual toleration, that is, in the absence of a hot war. It is a well-known fact, however, that the more intense political struggles become in time of crisis the greater the danger of universal concepts and even of ordinary propaganda acquiring traits of an armed doctrine. Thus during emergencies, in time of war, the United States' range of behavior—as well as of states that are underpinned by a secular conception of politics and have only in exceptional times invoked universal concepts to degrade an adversary—has oscillated between an almost non-ideological conception of politics, one that conceives an adversary as an enemy, to an almost "total conception of ideology" (Mannheim),[3] one that views an opponent somewhat short of a foe.[4]

On the level of ideas both Woodrow Wilson and Franklin Roosevelt have come close to a foe conception of politics. Wilson's ideal of making the world "safe for democracy" and Roosevelt's "four freedoms"—freedom to worship God, freedom of speech, freedom from fear, and freedom from want—possessed ingredients of a crusading spirit and thus lent themselves to being translated into militant doctrines of action. On the other hand, however, Wilson declared on January 22, 1917 that the peace to be concluded after World War I would have to be one "without victory," for "victory would mean peace forced upon the loser, a victor's terms imposed upon the vanquished." In his Fourteen Points speech on January 8, 1918 Wilson reiterated this classical notion of what peace is all about in the epoch of the modern European sovereign state. He declared then that "we wish [Germany] only to accept a place of equality among the peoples of the world—the new world in which we now live—instead of a place of mastery."

Despite the bombastic ideals that were hurled from Washington across the ocean and the enormous quantity of blood that was spilled during the conflict, the war was largely waged within the parameters of the *jus publicum Europaeum,* that is, a war reflecting the traditional secular or nonideological conception of politics. Hostilities were generally confined to the combatants at the front, and relatively few civilians were either killed or wounded. With regard to World War II no one can really reproach the United States for not having behaved correctly on land and for not having treated prisoners of war in accordance with existing conventions. If the war were viewed, however, exclusively from the perspective of the fire raids over Germany and Japan and our use of two atomic bombs, the conclusion may be drawn that the "four freedoms," for example, had become transformed into a militant doctrine. But because any war has to be analyzed from every perspective, it seems to me that the overall United States conduct during World War II continued on balance to reflect a secular or nonideological conception of politics and the adversary was thus still treated largely as an enemy.[5]

But there can be no question that the traditional conception of politics had by then received mortal blows. In fact, the tilt toward the "ideologization" of politics had already occurred toward the end of World War I. The Russian Revolution and the Treaty of Versailles were the decisive turning points.

The Revolution and the Soviet decision to withdraw from the conflict brought the Bolsheviks face to face with the representatives of the Central Powers at Brest-Litovsk. The negotiations clearly revealed the two contrasting conceptions of politics, the traditional secular notion and politics dominated by an ideology. Whereas the Central Powers were concerned with what they understood to be interests of state, that is, their aims, however great, were, nevertheless, limited in scope, the Bolsheviks, on the contrary, were mainly concerned with spreading Marxist-Leninist ideology. The Central Powers, according to John Wheeler-Bennett, "thought in terms of strategic lines, of provinces ceded, of economic advantages to be gained" and "spoke the ancient language of diplomacy, time-honoured and crusted with tradition." The Bolsheviks, on the other hand, were not much concerned about "frontiers and concessions." They used the meetings

> as a sounding-board for the propagation of their doctrine. In their principles of a general European peace they were not concerned with geographical terms and expressions. They banked upon the immediate effect of their propaganda on the war-weary masses of Europe to achieve what they knew could not be achieved by force of arms, namely the World Revolution and the replacement of Imperialism by 'the rule of the proletariat.'[6]

Although the Versailles settlement was not as momentous as the Russian Revolution, it did, nevertheless, have repercussions that too were global. The case of Versailles is an example of the momentum that propaganda can acquire. Even though the war was still largely waged within the parameters of the *jus publicum Europaeum,* Article 231 of the treaty, the so-called war guilt clause for example, was ideologically suggestive.

As is well known, an assumption on which the *jus publicum Europaeum* rests is that a state of peace must be clearly distinguished from that of war (*inter pacem et bellum nihil est medium*). According to this order every war between sovereign states had to be resolved by a genuine peace, that is, one in which the vanquished state is fully reintegrated into the community of states and permitted to function as a sovereign and equal entity. Yet Article 231 charging Germany with aggression contravened this assumption. Among the implications that this war guilt clause had was that Germans are criminals, morally bankrupt, inferior, and outcasts of humanity. The victors rationalized their policy of keeping Germany weak and apart from the civilized world once it was demoted morally. Winston Churchill aptly reflected the mood of the victors when he stated that "Germany may take the first step toward the ultimate reunion with the civilized world . . . by combatting Bolshevism [and] by being the bulwark against it."[7]

The contamination of politics with ideology as happened with the Communist victory in 1917, the conception of politics on which Imperial Japan already rested, as Arthur Tiedemann has shown, the moral expulsion of Germany, and subsequently Hitler's accession to power in 1933, a result of Versailles, undermined the traditional *jus publicum Europaeum*. The spread of ideologies[8] on a global scale overshadowed by far the period of the French Revolution and the Napoleonic wars.

That political entities with distinct conceptions of politics generally operate in different political currents cannot be denied. Yet it would be an oversimplification to assert that every ideologically motivated totalitarian one-party state necessarily injects ideology into foreign policy. Not all such political entities need by definition possess militant ideologies of a global scope. But for those that do, and for ideology to be effectively translated into foreign policy, that is, without its turning into empty rhetoric, hinges primarily on the power's total resources in being rather than potential and, second, on the configuration of the political forces in the world.

Nazi Germany and Soviet Russia offer two examples of political powers propelled by ideologies of a world scope. Although the former approached the matter of realizing its ideological goal differently from that of the Soviet Union, there are, nevertheless, some similarities. With regard to Nazi Germany, ideology, as John Herz has shown, was inextricably linked to the person of Hitler.

Although always mindful of the ideological goal to be realized, Hitler did not initially permit this to blind him to his and Germany's necessary order of priorities. Thus upon his accession to power he addressed himself to the immediate problems as he perceived them, namely, the solidification of his power and the revitalization of Germany. To accomplish this he moved simultaneously in a number of directions, including the elimination of political opposition, the unification of the German people by synchronizing them to his *Weltanschauung*, reviving Germany's economy, and strengthening the *Reichswehr*. While still involved in solidifying his powers and invigorating Germany, he could not afford to incur the wrath of the outside world, particularly that of France. Fearing outside intervention, he deemed it wise at the outset to underplay his ideology abroad and hence he packaged Germany as a peace-loving state, one that was wronged at Versailles. Translated into foreign policy this meant tearing up the remnants of the Versailles settlement. In this context he staked out Germany's right to rearm and to some limited territorial acquisitions.

Hitler's posture had the desired effect, particularly in Great Britain. The British dismissed his ideology at home as largely rhetoric, and Germany's ambitions abroad were perceived as reflecting her national interests and, therefore, not contravening the traditional notion of limited interests of state and, as such, mainly in accord with the *jus publicum Europaeum*. The politically moderate image that Britain entertained of Germany, to an extent as late as Munich and even after, was responsible for its failure to forge in time a common policy with at least France against Nazi Germany.

In the midst of the divisiveness between France and England that he helped to fuel Hitler succeeded in molding Germany into the foremost political power on the Continent, poised to embark on the road to ideological fulfillment. The concrete signal came with Germany's dismemberment of rump Czechoslovakia in March 1939, the first territory of non-German-speaking people that he occupied.

After this bloodless success Hitler was eager to proceed. Still anxious to avoid a direct confrontation with the Soviet Union or possibly a joint British-French-Russian conflict,

Hitler reached an ideologically incongruous but tactically sound accommodation with his arch foe Stalin. The secret clauses of the Ribbentrop-Molotov pact of August 1939 divided Eastern Europe into a German and Soviet sphere of influence that included an anticipated partition of Poland along the line of the rivers Narew, Vistula, and San. This pact enabled Germany to go to war against Poland with the certainty that Hitler would not be confronted by a major two-front conflict.

The Nazi-Soviet pact, the attack on Poland, and even Hitler's conduct of the war until June 1941 still displayed a sense of caution on his part. From Germany's perspective it can be argued that eliminating some enemies and foes piecemeal was sound military policy, a policy that Germany's resources were able to sustain. But it was sometime during this phase of the war, between September 1939 and June 1941, that Hitler lost sight of reality. His decision in the second half of 1940 to launch an invasion of the Soviet Union in the following year, even though Britain had not been knocked out of the war and the power potential of the United States had not yet been brought decisively to bear on Germany, betrayed a drastically curtailed ability to evaluate objectively the power-political forces in the world. Germany simply lacked the resources to sustain a major military forward thrust to implement Hitler's long-range goal that included Lebensraum and the extirpation of Bolshevism and Jewry. For, among other reasons, conquests in the East were apparently deemed necessary by Hitler to give "pure bred" Germany more space in which to raise the "new man" and create a large and solid springboard for further conquests.

Hitler's invasion of the Soviet Union in June 1941 and his declaration of war on the United States in December of that year mark the beginning of the end of the Third Reich. It appears to me that sometime between the decisive battles at El Alamein, Stalingrad, and Kursk, Hitler must have begun to perceive that he had overreached himself militarily. By accepting this hypothesis one can perhaps explain why it made no sense from his perspective to change the conduct of the war midstream. After all, from the very beginning he waged a purely ideological war in the East, and because military victory was becoming ever more elusive, it made sense from his point of view to implement at least his most easily attainable goal, namely, the extirpation of millions of Jews in territories that he still controlled directly. Thus the policy that resulted in wasting vital manpower, although economically and militarily counterproductive, was immaterial to him.

In contrast to Nazi Germany, the case of the Soviet Union is more complicated to judge because it is still an ongoing example. Nevertheless a sufficient amount of evidence is available that can enable one to establish a pattern of behavior that is to an extent reminiscent of Hitler's Germany.

For as long as the Soviet leadership was not solidly entrenched and was engaged in cleansing the country of alleged political opponents in the 1920s and 1930s and simultaneously was laying new economic and industrial foundations that would eventually be able to sustain the needs of a modern twentieth century political entity of its size, the Soviet Union was in no position to translate Marxist-Leninist doctrines into foreign policy. Hence its political posture in the interwar period is comparable to that of Nazi Germany until Hitler felt ready to implement his ideological schemes.

Since World War II the Soviet Union has again failed to approach a global status comparable to the one Hitler's Germany enjoyed on the Continent in the late 1930s and early 1940s. The United States, the greatest bastion of capitalism, is still a formidable power that the Soviet Union cannot simply wish away. Its relations with Communist China, a growing nuclear power, continue to be acerbic, and Soviet ties with its satellites are no longer as solid as they were previously. Domestically, too, the Soviet Union is beset by problems that Hitler did not face, including political dissension and lagging economic, technological, and industrial know-how. The Soviet Union also faces the specter of nationalism.

Given the political and military constellations in the world since World War II, on the one hand, and Marxist-Leninist doctrines, on the other hand, the powerholders in Moscow have proceeded cautiously in the international arena of politics just as Hitler did until the late 1930s. The political realism that has characterized Soviet behavior has given rise to a school of thought that believes that the ideological components in its politics are little else than empty rhetoric and that its foreign policy objectives are very much akin to those of pre-Soviet Russia. It appears that the proponents of this thesis equate appearance with essence exactly as the appeasers did with Hitler until he proved them wrong.

If the ideological components in Soviet foreign policy have largely been dismissed by power realists, one can no longer deny, however, that the question of ideology is now acute. In the face of the Soviet Union's current attempt to gain qualitative military parity with the United States, and indications are that she is in fact striving to gain military preponderance,[9] Vojtech Mastny correctly asked whether this development is indicative of a "drive for worldwide attainment of the ideological tenets of Marxism?"

Mastny's question raises another one: What does military superiority imply in the context of Communist ideology in this nuclear age? For an answer one must turn first to Khrushchev's reassessment of the Marxist-Leninist doctrine on the inevitability of war. According to him, "this precept was evolved at a time when (1) imperialism was an all-embracing world system, and (2) the social and political forces which did not want war were weak, poorly organized, and hence unable to compel imperialists to renounce war."[10] But in view of the changes favoring communism and because of the nuclear dimension, war, Khrushchev noted, is no longer "fatalistically inevitable."[11]

> There can be no doubt that a world nuclear war, if started by the imperialist maniacs, would inevitably result in the downfall of the capitalist system, a system breeding wars. But would the socialist countries and the cause of socialism all over the world benefit from a world nuclear disaster? Only people who deliberately shut their eyes to the facts can think so. As regards Marxist-Leninists, they cannot propose to establish a communist civilization on the ruins of centers of world culture, on land laid waste and contaminated by nuclear fallout. We need hardly add that in the case of many peoples, the question of socialism would be eliminated altogether because they would have disappeared bodily from our planet.[12]

The repudiation of war as a means of achieving the goal did not mean for Khrushchev that capitalism and communism could genuinely coexist as is the case, for example, between the United States and Japan and between France and West Germany. He consistently maintained that peaceful coexistence was not tantamount to accepting capitalism. The nuclear dimension merely made it necessary to intensify the struggle in the economic and other domains.[13] For example, reminiscent of Lenin was Khrushchev's insistence that the working people in capitalist countries contribute to the demise of capitalism by mastering "the use of *all forms* of struggle—peaceful and nonpeaceful, parliamentary and extra-parliamentary."[14] "Just war[s] of liberation"[15] and "sacred struggle[s] for . . . freedom"[16] must also be supported by the Soviet Union, not as ends in themselves but as beneficial tactics in wearing down and undermining capitalist states further.[17]

Although Khrushchev is now a nonperson in the pantheon of the Soviet Union, the tone that he set in the post-Stalin period has been followed by those that have succeeded him. With but minor variations on a theme, the proceedings of the 24th and 25th Communist party congresses read as if they could have taken place during his leadership rather than in the 1970s.[18] Continuity of policy[19] can also be seen in the instance of Khrushchev's intervention in Hungary and Brezhnev's occupation of Czechoslovakia. Support of so-called just and sacred struggles for liberation continues to be a cornerstone of Soviet policy. Exploiting the Middle East conflict as a means of undermining the West is also a significant feature in the Soviet Union's struggle against its class foe.

But the question remains: If all-out war is repudiated as a way of overcoming capitalism, why is the Soviet Union arming itself to the extent that it is?

Despite the fact that both Moscow and Washington appear at least now sincerely committed to avoiding a hot confrontation, the Soviet Union cannot rule out the possibility of war with the United States, particularly if the balance of power were to tilt drastically in Moscow's favor. Once it is perceived to be inferior, the United States may deem it necessary to restore some semblance of power parity. Conversely, a weakened Soviet Union may also decide to deliver a blow to the most powerful bastion of capitalism. All-out war can also come about accidentally. In addition to the ever present possibility of an East-West conflict, the Soviet Union is also propelled to arm itself to the extent that it does because of a fear of a possible conflict with Communist China. Such a possibility may confront the Soviet Union with a two-front war—against China and the NATO countries. A further Soviet calculation in arming itself so extensively may arise from the unreliability of some of its satellites in Eastern Europe. Keeping large forces there serves to remind the people that fundamental doctrinal deviations cannot be tolerated by Moscow. Although half forgotten in the West, Hungary and Czechoslovakia, among other examples, are well remembered in the East.

Thus there can be no question that power-political considerations are central to the Soviet Union's calculations. It so happens, however, that arming itself so extensively also fits tidily into the ideological framework within which the Kremlin operates. From Moscow's perspective Soviet military hegemony, if not challenged, may lead to the neutralization and Finlandization of a good part of the globe, a precondition for the realization of the much sought after ideological goal. Based on the cautiousness with which the Soviet Union is still proceeding diplomatically, despite its imposing military posture, one can only assume that its leaders are mindful of the dangers inherent in military conquests, particularly those that are ideologically motivated and may know no reasonable limits. Hitler's rule serves as an ever present reminder. Although his early military ventures were limited in scope, he escalated the conflict in 1941 into an ideological crusade in the east that ended in the rubble of Berlin.

NOTES

1. Karl Mannheim, *Ideology and Utopia: An Introduction to the Sociology of Knowledge,* trans. Louis Wirth and Edward Shils (New York, 1936), p. 57.

2. *Ibid.*

3. *Ibid.,* pp. 57, 59.

4. For a discussion of the conceptual distinction inherent in the words "enemy" and "foe" and for some of the political implications of this distinction, see George Schwab's "Enemy oder Foe: Der Konflikt der modernen Politik," tr. J. Zeumer, *Epirrhosis: Festagbe für Carl Schmitt,* ed. H. Barion *et at.* (Berlin, 1968), II, pp. 665-682. See also Ion X. Contiades, " 'ΕΧΘΡΟΣ' und 'ΠΟΛΕΜΙΟΣ' in der modernen politischen Theorie und der griechischen Antike," *Griechische Humanistische Gesellschaft,* Zweite Reihe (Athens, 1969), pp. 5ff.

5. The irregular nature of the Vietnam conflict, in particular the large-scale resort on the part of the Vietnamese to guerrilla warfare, must be viewed in the context of civil war. Such wars know no rules

and regulations.

6. John W. Wheeler-Bennett, *Brest-Litovsk: The Forgotten Peace, March 1918* (New York, 1966), p. 115. See also Arno J. Mayer, *Political Origins of the New Diplomacy, 1917-1918* (New York, 1970), pp. 293-312.

7. *The Times* (London), April 12, 1919.

8. In a penetrating study of the concept of ideology and Marxist theory, Peter C. Ludz defines ideology as "derived from an historically conditioned primary experience. It is a dogmatic and didactic combination of symbol-laden theoretical suppositions by which specific historical-social groups mediate a consciously utopian, tendentially closed and therefore distorted view of man, society, and the world—a view programatically and voluntaristically organized on the basis of a rigorous friend-foe polarization for a particular socio-political activity." *Ideologiebegriff und marxistische Theorie: Ansätze zu einer immanenten Kritik* (Opladen, 1976), p. 85. Because Ludz considers Hitlerism to have been "irrational," "capricious," a reaction against communist Russia, and the "failure of conservatism and liberalism," his definition is unfortunately not sufficiently broad to embrace National Socialism and hence he dismisses it as nonideological. *Ibid.*, pp. 84, 85.

9. For discussions of the Soviet effort in the military field, see the various publications of the International Institute for Strategic Studies at London, particularly the latest issues of *The Military Balance* and *Strategic Survey*.

10. N.S. Khrushchev, "From the 'Report' of the Central Committee of the Communist Party of the Soviet Union to the Twentieth Party Congress" (February 14, 1956), *On Peaceful Coexistence, A Collection* (Moscow, 1961), pp. 8-9.

11. *Ibid.*, p. 10.

12. *The New Content of Peaceful Coexistence in the Nuclear Age, Speech by N.S. Khrushchev at the 6th Congress of the Socialist Unity Party of Germany, Berlin, January 16, 1963* (New York, 1963), p. 34.

13. Khrushchev, "From the 'Report' of the Central Committee," *On Peaceful Coexistence*, p. 7.

14. See *Program of the Communist Party of the Soviet Union, Adopted by the 22nd Congress of the C.P.S.U., October 31, 1961* (New York, 1961), p. 45.

15. *The Present International Situation and the Foreign Policy of the Soviet Union, Report by N.S. Khrushchev to the USSR Supreme Soviet, December 12, 1962* (New York, 1963), p. 32.

16. *Ibid.*, p. 37.

17. *Program of the Communist Party . . .*, p. 43. See also N.S.

Khrushchev's "For New Victories of the Communist Movement, On Results of the Conference of Representatives of Communist and Workers' Parties," Reprinted in *The Current Digest of the Soviet Press,* vol. XIII, No. 4, February 22, 1961, pp. 12-13, also *Program of the Communist Party . . .* (1961), p. 43.

18. For some interesting reading, see, for example, A. Yakovlev, "The Ideological Struggle Today and Some Aspects of Ideological Work in the Light of the 24th C.P.S.U. Congress," *On Current Ideological Struggle* (Moscow, 1973), pp. 6-7, 34-35, also in the same volume V. Mshvenieradze, "Current Aspects of the Ideological Struggle in the Light of the 24th C.P.S.U. Congress," pp. 89-91. The August 1976 issue of the Moscow published journal *International Affairs* contains a series of illuminating articles under the title "The Present Stage in the General Crisis of Capitalism and World Revolution," pp. 3-50.

19. On the continuous struggle against the international bourgeoisie, see "Speech by L.I. Brezhnev, General Secretary of the C.P.S.U. Central Committee, Head of the C.P.S.U. Delegation, [Berlin,] June 29, 1976" in *For Peace, Security, Cooperation and Social Progress in Europe* (Moscow, 1976), pp. 21-27 and M. Suslov, "Our Epoch is an Epoch of the Triumph of Marxism-Leninism" in *Socialism, Theory and Practice* (Moscow, 1976), pp. 31-33. This is a reprint in the August 1976 issue in the *Soviet Monthly Digest* of an article that appeared originally in the No. 5 issue of *Kommunist* (1976).

Notes on Contributors

SEWERYN BIALER is a professor of political science at Columbia University and is acting director of its Research Institute on International Change. A Columbia University Ph.D., Professor Bialer's publications include *Stalin and His Generals.*

RENÉ ALBRECHT-CARRIÉ is professor emeritus at Barnard College and Columbia University, where he was also associated with the School of International Affairs. A Columbia University Ph.D., he has been a Fulbright lecturer in Italy and the recipient of a Guggenheim fellowship as well as of Rockefeller and Ford grants. His publications include *A Diplomatic History of Europe Since the Congress of Vienna.*

LLOYD C. GARDNER is a professor of history at Rutgers College, Rutgers University. A University of Wisconsin Ph.D., Professor Gardner has also taught in England. His major publication in the field of cold war history is *Architects of Illusion: Men and Ideas in American Foreign Policy, 1941-1949.*

JOHN H. HERZ is a professor of political science at The City College of New York and a member of the doctoral faculty at The City University Graduate School. A University of Cologne Ph.D., he has also taught at Columbia, The Fletcher School of Law and Diplomacy, The Graduate Faculty of The New School for Social Research, and in Germany. His most recent book is entitled *The Nation-State and the Crisis of World Politics.*

HAROLD C. HINTON is a professor of political science and international affairs at the Institute for Sino-Soviet Studies, The George Washington University. Professor Hinton received his Ph.D. from Harvard University and was a Social Science Research Council Research Training Fellow and a Fulbright Senior Research Scholar. A senior staff member of the Institute for Defense Analyses, his publications include *Three and a Half Powers: The New Balance in Asia.*

VOJTECH MASTNY is a professor of history at the University of Illinois. He received his Ph.D. from Columbia University, where he has also taught and served as acting director of its Institute on East Central Europe. The recipient of a Lehrman Institute grant and a Guggenheim award, his forthcoming book is entitled *Russia's Road to the Cold War: Stalin's War Aims, 1941-1945.*

HANS J. MORGENTHAU is University Professor of Political Science at The Graduate Faculty of The New School for Social Research. A University of Frankfurt J.U.D., Professor Morgenthau has taught at the universities of Geneva, Chicago, Columbia, Harvard, Yale, The City College of New York and The City University Graduate School. A consultant to the Department of State, he is also chairman of the National Committee on American Foreign Policy. His publications include *Politics Among Nations.*

ARTHUR M. SCHLESINGER, JR. is Albert Schweitzer Professor of the Humanities at The City University Graduate School. Educated at Harvard and Cambridge, Professor Schlesinger taught at Harvard University before becoming special assistant to President Kennedy. Professor Schlesinger is a member of the Council on Foreign Relations. He has won the Pulitzer prize twice. Among his publications is *The Imperial Presidency.*

GEORGE SCHWAB is a professor of history at The City College of New York and a member of the doctoral faculty at The City University Graduate School. He received the Ph.D. from Columbia University and has also taught there. A member of the Executive Board of the National Committee on American Foreign Policy, Professor Schwab is the recipient of several grants from the Research Foundation of The City University of New York. His most recent publication is a translation of Carl Schmitt's *The Concept of the Political.*

ARTHUR E. TIEDEMANN is a professor of history and chairman of the department at The City College of New York, City University. He received the Ph.D. from Columbia University and teaches there as a visiting professor of Japanese history. Among his publications is *Modern Japan: A Brief History.*

DONALD S. ZAGORIA is a professor of political science at Hunter College, City University, and a member of the doctoral faculty at The City University Graduate School. He received the Ph.D. from Columbia University where he is also a Fellow of its Research Institute on International Change. A member of the Editorial Board of *Comparative Politics,* his publications include *The Sino-Soviet Conflict.*

Index

162

Index